Endorsements for Captain Andy Miller's
Holistic Hospitality

Since my early days with The Salvation Army I have watched the debate between the practical hands-on social work of the Army and the spiritual dimension of our work. What is the proper balance between soup, soap, and salvation? General John Gowans referenced the Army's mission as a three-legged stool: saving souls, growing saints and serving suffering humanity. The stool cannot stand when not supported by all three legs. General John Larsson explained the balanced ministry by likening it to a butterfly with two wings, social and spiritual. The butterfly cannot fly when only one wing is operational. I am pleased to endorse this new work by Captain Andrew Miller III, a casework model, demonstrating the holistic ministry of The Salvation Army.

Donald C. Bell, Commissioner
Territorial Commander
USA Southern Territory

The practice of hospitality is more than just a theory for Captain Andy Miller. It is part of his heritage and DNA. It was through such practice of hospitality that his grandmother, Commissioner Joan Miller, was welcomed by Salvation Army officers, which launched her own mission of hospitality. Andy's legendary grandfather, Commissioner Andy Miller, never met a stranger and was able to minister to heads of state like President Ronald Reagan as well as the poor homeless person on skid row. I have seen firsthand the mission of hospitality that Captains Andy and Abby Miller instituted in the Arlington, Texas, Corps, which resulted in meeting both the temporal and eternal needs of people whom many in society had rejected.

David E. Jeffrey, Commissioner
National Commander

The issue is perennial: melding our many programs into a vital whole that makes the welcoming embrace of the Father's love believable. Whether and how we see the stranger makes all the difference. Captain Andrew Miller III here makes a compelling case for adopting the Biblical metaphor of hospitality as central to understanding our life and mission in the Army. He ably grounds the issue in the Scripture story, our Army history and the realities engaging our corps and service programs in community. More than theory, what he proposes is practical, provocative and potentially transformative. This is a priority read for Salvationists, employees and advisory board members, particularly in local corps settings.

General Paul A. Rader (Ret.)
Lexington, Kentucky

Early in my Christian walk I would have told you that hospitality was not on my list of gifts or capacities. Why? Because I was not the best at matching the napkins with the centerpiece or planning the right menu for each occasion. But then I learned that this thing called "hospitality" was so much more. Freedom in Christ opened the door for me to love inviting people to the 'table.' Jesus says, even today, "Go out to the roads and country lanes and make them come in, so that my house will be full." (Luke 14:23-24) And as his servant I want to know and act on the belief that "there is still room." (Luke 14:22b) That's what Captain Andy is telling us—imploring us, to embrace.

Globally, our Army is resonating with his challenge to us. Personally, I respond because I know the author is the real thing. He lives this concept out in his whole life. He learned it from his mom and dad. It's incarnational. He makes me feel welcome and "at home." And isn't that what we want, more people at His table?

Sue Swanson, Commissioner
Territorial President, Women's Ministries
USA Eastern Territory
West Nyack, New York

Holistic Hospitality invites the reader to both become a participant in the process of missional renewal at the Family Life Center in Arlington and to learn important leadership lessons along with the author Captain Andy Miller. Replete with clear teaching on the biblical imperative of the practice of hospitality, a healthy dose of Salvation Army history, and a cast of earthy characters, *Holistic Hospitality* will challenge Salvationists to revisit the purpose of and approach to housing ministries. Don't finish this book without stepping into Andy's shoes as a homeless man asks him, "Yeah, Cap, what is a metaphor?"

Captain Marion Platt, III
Divisional Youth Secretary
Florida Division, USA
Tampa, Florida

Around the world, the church is challenged today to be relevant while also being faithful to God. Andy Miller grapples with this challenge and offers a way forward—be hospitable. Miller's book is an inspiring example of quality, rich, robust, readable, practical theology. There are many fascinating insights into the realities of ministry in Arlington—real people facing real problems seeking faithful responses. Miller is easy to read but don't be fooled: his excellent proposals for the way forward for the whole Salvation Army—whether based in corps, centre, community or headquarters—are built on distilled, cutting-edge, contemporary theology. Read, reflect, and then do it!

Dean Pallant, Major
Under Secretary for Program Resources
and International Health Services Coordinator
International Headquarters
London, England

Andy Miller III

Foreword by General André Cox

The Salvation Army
USA Southern Territory
Literary Council
1424 Northeast Expressway
Atlanta, GA 30329

ISBN: 978-0-86544-080-7

Editor: Linda D. Johnson, The WordWorking Shop
Illustrator: Laura Kelly

Printed in the United States of America

In memory of my grandfathers:

Major Roy Tompkins (1925-2005). His life and ministry had a dramatic shift when he experienced the holistic hospitality of the Kingdom through the Army's ministry as a young man. As a result he became a stalwart preacher of the Gospel and a sterling example for my life.

Commissioner Andy Miller, Sr. (1923-2011), whose effervescent life challenged me to see the power of a "balanced ministry" that is holistically hospitable. This book is in many ways an expansion of his famous mantra, seen in my memory as he clasped his hands above his head: "When we do our ministry right [social and spiritual] you can't tell the two apart."

Table of Contents

FOREWORD

In a recently televised interview I was asked: "How is social work in The Salvation Army enhancing evangelism in Army ministry?" My immediate response was that the question should have been put around the other way, or perhaps even asked differently: "How does our spiritual and God-given calling to preach the message of transformation in Christ impact the Salvation Army's social work?" Captain Andrew Miller III gets to the heart of this challenge in his book, *Holistic Hospitality*.

Salvationists around the world have heard me say that I dream of an Army "rooted and confident in the Word of God." Captain Miller's presentation of holistic hospitality has a firm foundation in Scripture. If we take the Bible to heart, we will implement the Apostle Paul's exhortation to "Practice hospitality." (Romans 12:16) Captain Miller's holistic vision is similarly rooted in Church and Salvation Army history—in particular the Founder's passion for "salvation for both worlds."

With Captain Miller, I dream of an Army that "reflects the mind of Jesus in our commitment to the poor and marginalised." We can no longer look at those who come to us as clients or cases, but rather as people created in God's image. Captain Miller's approach toward unleashing holistic hospitality in the ministry of a corps provides a refreshing way to unite Salvation Army advisory boards, soldiers, staff, and those we serve. Too often, our relationships to these stakeholders can be somewhat fragmented. When they are all brought together, as Captain Miller did at his corps in Arlington, Texas, the result is eye-opening for each group and yields powerful results for the Kingdom as everyone unites behind a common vision of true Christian hospitality.

In all that we do, I pray that we will not be primarily concerned about the reputation of The Salvation Army; that we will not preach about ourselves but instead work tirelessly to "practice hospitality" through the way we offer welcome to all. When we do that, we are proclaiming the message of Jesus, who alone brings freedom, hope and life

General André Cox
International Leader of The Salvation Army

ACKNOWLEDGMENTS

This project has been brewing for several years. The light bulb went off as I participated in Dr. Christine Pohl's course, "The Ethics of Hospitality," at Asbury Theological Seminary.

Originally I had an audience of three in mind for this book: Dr. Elaine Heath, Dr. Billy Abraham, and Major Ward Matthews, my dissertation committee at SMU-Perkins. My thanks to each of them for their encouragement, helpful critiques and support.

As I wrote the original project I had three dialogue partners who read every line and helped sharpen my argument: Professor Yvonne Moulton, Dr. R. David Rightmire, and my father–in–law, Dr. Don Adams. Also General Shaw Clifton, Major Stephen Court, Dr. Howard Snyder and Dr. Steven O'Malley gave helpful comments regarding the original manuscript. Dr. Roger Green (OF) and Dr. Jonathan Raymond published a shorter paper in Word & Deed and have often encouraged my writing.

The Salvationist faculty at Asbury University, Drs. Ron and Bea Holz (OF), Dr. Ed McKinley, Professor James Curnow, and General Dr. Paul Rader all invested significant time by listening to my questions and helping me mature as a scholar and soldier.

Others too should be mentioned: Commissioner David Jeffrey, Major Dean Pallant, Captain Zach Bell, Captain Marion Platt III, Commissioners Barry and Sue Swanson, Commissioners Don and

Debi Bell, Commissioner Phil Needham, Lt. Colonels Henry and Doris Gonzalez, Joann Johnson, Dixon Holman, Martin Jackson, Cynthia Ard, and Bill Myers.

While attending Booth Academy (my parents' name for our home school), Majors Andy (Jr.) and Cheryl Miller ignited my passion for The Salvation Army's mission. My classmates there—Captain Diana James, Professor Nathan Miller, and Karen Miller—helped me work out my understanding of a Christian identity in a dynamic community.

I offer my deep appreciation to the people of The Salvation Army of Arlington whose commitment to God's mission for the Army is unflinching. My area commanders while serving in Arlington, Majors Mark and Susan Brown and Majors Ward and Michelle Matthews, each gave outstanding support to my educational efforts and, consequently, this book.

Colonel Brad Bailey and the Southern Territory's Literary Council have been instrumental in moving this project from dissertation to book. Linda Johnson's guidance and expertise helped me transform this formal academic project into a book that more effectively reaches my intended audience.

Every time I use the first-person pronoun in this book, I could be wrong. Army officership for me has developed as a team effort with my wife, Abby. From my research to practical application, every layer of this book assumes the "we" of our teamwork and our partnership in the fight. In that spirit I thank Captain Abby Miller for the significant role she plays in this book. To Abby, Andy IV, Titus Wesley, and Georgia Kay, thanks for the joy and encouragement you regularly give to me. I am proud to be a part of "team Miller" and to lead you "forward to the fight." There are some great titles in my life but outside of being a follower of Christ my favorite titles are husband and Daddy.

INTRODUCTION

For several years, I have been attracted to the Christian practice of hospitality. I have preached on hospitality; Chapter 1 of this book is one of those messages. I have taught on hospitality. I have encouraged people to understand their outreach through the lens of hospitality. But I had not implemented a plan to renew a Salvation Army ministry in light of hospitality until I was corps officer, with my wife, Abby, at Arlington, Texas.

Like most corps officers in the United States, I was responsible for leading four distinct groups that were unconnected to one another: the congregation, the advisory council, the staff, and the people served through the corps' ministry. Navigating this diversity had been a challenge for my leadership. So I set out to unite these groups with the goal of renewing Arlington's transitional housing ministry. The project was the basis for my dissertation in pursuit of a Doctorate of Ministry degree from Southern Methodist University's Perkins School of Theology.

When I first began conceptualizing the project, I admit I was focused on how I could "change the Army." I naively demanded that systematic change in the Army's approach to "social ministry" should come by means of evaluating its history, and I brashly was going to accomplish this through my project.

If I had the opportunity to talk with the General and present my concept, I reasoned in an imaginary scenario, it could be implemented by executive order. But even if that happened, I had to ask whether real change in the praxis could be refreshed in the battle of the Army's daily fight. What if the next General decided that he or she didn't care for this plan? And what about individual Salvation Army officers like me—would they connect to a vision handed down through multiple layers of Army administration? As I evaluated my leadership in the local corps and my scholarly research interest over the past five years, I was reminded that the goal of my project should not be to implement such macrocosmic change.

While such a lofty goal might demonstrate my commitment to and concern for the Army as a whole, I soon came to realize that such sweeping change is beyond my control. I also realized that I must first apply my ideas to my own particular setting, a place where I could have some real influence. If this concept of hospitality could help The Salvation Army in Arlington be more missional, then it would have a chance of impacting local leadership in Army units around the world. Renewed theological praxis can happen only if I take action myself in areas that I can influence for the Kingdom.

So I start out by looking at how the practice of hospitality is rooted in Scripture and tradition (Chapter 2). Then I examine the Salvation Army's historical and theological background and analyze the evolution of Salvation Army ministry from its founding by William Booth. That examination leads me to propose that eschatology—the part of theology concerned with the last things—is the primary way of understanding Booth's theology. Booth's eschatology, in my view, was the theological engine that enabled Booth and his Army to enlarge their capacity for developing various programs that would later develop into housing ministries such as the family shelter in Arlington (Chapter 3).

Next, I aim to establish a foundation for renewing the theological praxis of this housing ministry. I suggest that bifurcating, or separating, our "social" and "spiritual" ministries stands in the way of the Army's ability to act upon its holistic heritage (Chapter 4). I also suggest that the Christian tradition and practice of hospitality can serve as a preferable paradigm to "social services." I believe that the early Salvation Army presents our contemporary Army—and the Christian church in general—with a prophetic social ethic that has hospitality at its core. This legacy of hospitality and holistic ministry can serve as a lens by which the contemporary Army looks to the future (Chapter 5).

Based upon my research, I designed a model project that has the potential to reconnect a robust ministry to its historic and hospitable roots.

There were three phases of the project. In the first phase, I met with a task force to design a curriculum for a three–hour "educational session" that would involve people from all the constituencies of Arlington's ministry (Chapter 6). The task force helped to structure the educational session and select who would be invited (Chapter 7). The second phase was inviting people to the session, where participants learned about the concept of hospitality and its biblical, theological, and historical roots; toured the Family Life Center; then brainstormed ideas to refresh the shelter (Chapters 8 and 9). In the third phase, three changes were implemented, and I looked at whether those changes had an effect on renewing the theological praxis of hospitality in our housing ministry (Chapter 10). Finally, I offer some reflections on the implications of the project both for my own ministry as a corps officer and for the Army as a whole (Chapter 11).

My prayer is that as you read, you will feel the power of hospitality that is truly missional. I believe that such hospitality is connected to God's plan to redeem the world and that The Salvation Army is in a perfect position to offer it.

My plea is that you, as a Salvation Army officer or influencer on Salvation Army mission working in a local setting, would be inspired by the Founder's vision, the history of our movement, and my humble project in Arlington to see hospitality as something you can embrace—and something you can use to embrace others in your own sphere of influence.

Chapter 1

Make Room

Love must be sincere. Hate what is evil; cling to what is good. Be devoted to one another in love. Honor one another above yourselves. Never be lacking in zeal, but keep your spiritual fervor, serving the Lord. Be joyful in hope, patient in affliction, faithful in prayer. Share with the Lord's people who are in need. Practice hospitality. —Romans 12:9–13

I wanted to leave, and no one would have blamed me. I could see nothing but an ocean of gold and dark blue. There had to be 40,000 people looking down at me, and not one was glad to see me. I was at the bottom of the section, and our tickets were marked NN, so our seats were far past the Z section, at least 40 rows away. As I looked up, my legs tightened for the climb ahead.

My parents, who were then serving a Salvation Army corps in St. Louis, had gotten us the tickets to see our team, the Chicago Bears, play the high–flying, "greatest show on turf," St. Louis Rams. But it was a Sunday game, and there was no way we were getting out of church early. So we arrived at the game in the middle of the second quarter. The fans were all in their seats as my family walked in. My brother and I, with our Bears jerseys and other fan gear on, tried to balance our food as we walked up the seemingly endless staircase. You can imagine the interesting and colorful language that was flying in our direction. Talk about feeling out of place! We wanted to leave, but we "hung in there" even in the face of defeat. I have never felt as unwelcomed by so many people as I did that day. People did not want to make room for us in their stadium.

Have you ever felt unwelcome? Your experience might not be as dramatic as being outnumbered by thousands at a football game. Maybe you moved to a new town or stepped into a new school. Maybe you were sent in to replace someone else on a job, or you had to give someone an assignment you knew they didn't want. Sometimes when people are forced to make room, they are not very welcoming.

Or have there been times when it was you who didn't want to make room? I grew up in a family with four kids (I was the oldest), so private space did not exist in our house. As most Salvationists know, the Army owns the houses of officers. On one occasion, we moved from a five-bedroom house to a three-bedroom one. Well, I did not want to give up my space and "make room" for my brother.

Sacrificing your space is hard. But "making room" is more than a physical reality. Maybe you don't want to make room in your world for people you don't like. Making room stinks. Why? Because you have to give up; you have to give in; and you have to share.

Reading Romans 12:9–13, it's easy to jump past some of the commands Paul gives. The text seems like a typical list of "do's" and don'ts." In just the first few verses we read: "Be devoted ... honor one another ... never lack in zeal ... keep your spiritual fervor ... be joyful in hope ... be patient ... be faithful in prayer ... share ... " The list is much like what my wife, Abby, and I said to our son, Andy IV, as he went off to pre-school. Suddenly we felt the need to summarize everything we had taught him in three years of life: "Ask for help, say please, eat your food, tell your teachers when you have to go ... " (Then we cried because we saw the inevitability of our son's growing up.)

After Paul's list of admonitions, he writes one command in a sentence that takes two words: "***Practice hospitality.***" The force in the original language is hard to communicate. In Greek, it is as if Paul underlined this word and made the font extra large, extra bold, with italics: "You ***must*** practice hospitality." Or it could be translated, "Pursue hospitality." The word here for *pursue* was often used to describe a hunt or a vigorous chase.

The backstory of this letter is that Paul was writing to Christians in Rome whom he had not met. The church there was not a big group that came together in a large cathedral. Instead, there were small churches that met in homes. What was distinct about this Christian population was that some were Christianized Jews and others were Gentile Christians. In 49 A.D., the Jews in Rome had been exiled, and this letter was likely written as they were returning from that exile. The two groups had to learn how to love each other and exist as "the church" in Rome. You can imagine that they might not have wanted to get along. Paul was giving them this command to practice hospitality because it was something that they lacked. He needed to say, "Be devoted to one another in love" (12:10), and "Share with the Lord's people who are in need." (12:13) Maybe these Christians needed to be challenged to make room for each other.

We live in a very inhospitable time. As a society, we don't want to make room for anything. We don't want to make room for others, especially strangers. Even though I meet strangers who are looking for help every day right here in my office, it is easy for me to say to myself, *Don't they realize that I am behind on a hundred emails, and our Angel Tree application process doesn't start for two weeks? Can't they read the sign on the door?* In our increasingly isolated world, it is also easy for us to stick with the friends we have on Facebook, the contacts in our email list, or the people we see on a regular basis. We don't have time for new people—for strangers.

But the heart of the word *hospitality* is *strangers*. In Greek, the word for hospitality is an invented word, kind of like "shop-ortunity" or "fan-demonium." It combines the word for brotherly love, *phileos* (as in

Philadelphia), and the word for stranger, *xenos*. The essence of the word hospitality, then, is "love of stranger."

Today, the word hospitality has come to be associated with the hospitality industry or conversation over coffee at someone's house. But until the last 300 years, the word was specifically understood as a Christian practice. So the root of the word, *hosp,* is found in the words *hospital, hostel,* and *hospice.* The idea was that Christians had a duty to make room for strangers.

Our inhospitable world, in which "it's all about me," shuts people out. That is why most Salvation Army shelters have a waiting list. It is why people are starving; it is why children are left alone; it is why people are sold into slavery; it is why there are wars.

Our lack of a welcoming attitude is more than, "We don't want to make room … We don't want to practice hospitality." The scary thought to me is that we often say to ourselves: "We don't *have* to make room … We don't *have* to practice hospitality … We don't *have* to love the stranger."

God didn't *have* to make room either. These problems in our world are not His fault. Sin is not His fault. God created our world for us, but our corporate sin in Adam has brought us to a place of rejecting all that God has given us. Our sin separates us from God; our selfishness keeps us from looking at anyone beyond ourselves; and those things that we know have moved against God's direction in our lives give God every right to say, "I don't have to make room."

But thanks be to God that in Jesus Christ, God made room for us. We don't deserve the mercy of God as He stepped out in time in the person of Jesus Christ to welcome us. When our world is blind and looking for its way, Jesus steps in as the Savior for all of humanity to offer us salvation— to save us from our sin, and to offer us a new way of understanding and looking at the world.

Later in Paul's letter, he challenges the believers in Rome to, "Welcome one another, then, just as Christ welcomed you, for the glory of God." (15:7, *NRSV*) How did Jesus welcome us? He welcomed us on the Cross. While I was a cadet at the training college in Atlanta, I often I went out on our canteen ministry, where we interacted with people living under bridges on a weekly basis. One man became my friend. He said to me one day, "I know why you do this, 'cause of what He [finger pointing up] did."

In other words, we help people not to make ourselves feel better but because Jesus has welcomed us.

I suggest that we would do well to reframe our ministry in The Salvation Army. We should not be simply "doing social services" or "opening a shelter." Instead we should be opening ourselves, our resources, and our buildings, as we are commanded to do, in light of Christ's making room for us. We should ***practice hospitality***.

Chapter 2

Hospitality: Rooted in Scripture and Tradition

Hospitality is more than offering rich desserts and making small talk with family and friends. It is not a spiritual gift for those who like to bake. On the contrary, through the Scriptures and church history, hospitality has been concerned with interaction among "others" and the practice of welcoming "strangers."

Weren't we strangers—in the sense of being estranged from God—when Jesus welcomed us? When he opened His arms to be nailed to the Cross, His sacrifice meant that He opened His arms to receive us. When we in turn received that welcome, we joined the fellowship of the triune God. The practice of hospitality finds its source and highest expression in the nature of this God, who continually welcomes humanity into the eternal fellowship of the Godhead.

Even before Jesus came, the theme of hospitality resonated in the Scriptures. The "big picture" of the Old Testament is the story of God's calling Abram and his people out of Ur to a foreign land where they were aliens; the Israelites' being taken captive into Egypt, another land where they were aliens; and their deliverance from slavery into Canaan, the land of promise, where they were outsiders. The Lord reminded the Israelites that though He had given the land into their hands, it did not belong to them. He said, " … you reside in my land as foreigners and strangers." (Lev. 25:23) When King David later thanked God that he and his people were able to provide so much for the building of the Temple, he prayed:

> But who am I, and who are my people, that we should be able to give as generously as this? Everything comes from you, and we have given you only what comes from your hand. We are foreigners and strangers in your sight, as were all our ancestors. Our days on earth are like a shadow, without hope. (1 Chronicles 29:14–15)

The Israelites, in their best moments, realized their utter dependence on God for everything they had. God also commanded them to express their gratefulness for His providence in how they treated others. The Lord said, "Do not oppress a foreigner; you yourselves know how it feels to be foreigners, because you were foreigners in Egypt." (Exodus 23:9) The Lord warned the Israelites not to mistreat foreigners but to treat them as "your native-born." (Leviticus 19:33)

The Lord emphasized to the Israelites that everything—"the heavens, even the highest heavens, the earth, and everything in it"—belonged to Him, yet he had "set his affection" on their ancestors, and on them. (Deuteronomy 10:14–15) This Lord offered abundant hospitality—to the Israelites and to those who came to live with them. "He defends the cause of the fatherless and the widow, and loves the foreigner residing among you, giving them food and clothing." (Deuteronomy 10:18) The Israelites also had a tribe among them, the Levites, who had been set apart for ministry, which meant that they had no way of earning money and that they had no inheritance other than the Lord Himself. (Deuteronomy 10:8–9) The Levites had to rely totally on the generosity— the hospitality—of the people for their sustenance.

The Lord decreed a very practical way that the Israelites should offer hospitality if they expected their own work to be blessed.

> *At the end of every three years, bring all the tithes of that year's produce and store it in your towns, so that the Levites (who have no allotment or inheritance of their own) and the foreigners, the fatherless, and the widows who live in your towns may come and eat and be satisfied, and so that the Lord your God may bless you in all the work of your hands.* (Deuteronomy 14:28–29)

The Lord's commands went beyond giving tithes to others. He also expected just treatment for everyone—paying hired workers a fair wage, for example, and not taking the cloak of a widow as collateral for a loan. The Lord told farmers not to harvest every last sheaf of grain or every last olive or grape but to leave some behind for foreigners, the fatherless, and widows to gather. With every command, the Lord reminded the Israelites that they should do these things because they remembered their own time of slavery in Egypt. (Deuteronomy 24:14–22)

Throughout the Old Testament, there are wonderful examples of people offering hospitality. What might have happened if Abraham and Sarah had not rolled out the red carpet for the "three men"—angels—who appeared to them at Mamre? It was only after a sumptuous feast prepared by Sarah that the men announced she would bear a child in about a year. (Genesis 18)

What might have happened if Rahab had not offered hospitality—a place to hide—to the two Israelite spies who came to Jericho? Because of her kindness, she and her family were spared when the city came down. (Joshua 2) And she would become one of five women listed in the genealogy of Jesus. (Matthew 1)

What might have happened to a widow and her son if she had not offered hospitality to the prophet Elijah? She gave everything she had—just a handful of flour and a little olive oil in a jug—and she fully expected to die. But miraculously, because of her sacrifice and generosity, the jar of flour was not used up and the jug of oil did not run dry. (1 Kings 17: 7–16)

In the New Testament, the teachings of Jesus powerfully encouraged people to show welcome toward others. Ethicist Christine Pohl, whose class on hospitality at Asbury Theological Seminary sparked my passion for the subject, suggests that Matthew 25 and Luke 14 are central in the formation and praxis of the tradition of hospitality.[1]

In Matthew 25, Jesus describes the end of days, when people will be separated into the "sheep" and the "goats." The "sheep" will be those who gave the King drink when he was thirsty, a place to stay when he was a stranger, clothing when he was in need, care when he was sick, and a visit when he was in prison. When the righteous ask when they have done such things for the King, he will reply, " 'Truly I tell you, whatever you did for one of the least of these brothers and sisters of mine, you did for me.' "

The parable of the great banquet recounted in Luke 14 describes a man who had prepared a feast, but all his invited guests begged off. So the man commanded his servants, " 'Go out quickly into the streets and alleys of the town and bring in the poor, the crippled, and the lame.' " When there was still room at the table, the master went even further, commanding his servants to go out to the lanes and country roads to find more guests.

This sounds very much like a parable for The Salvation Army. The world around us may be making excuses about coming to church, but there are many "guests" we are called to invite and seat with honor at our "table."

If such a clear injunction were not enough, we can also turn to some direct commands. The Apostle Paul says to the church at Rome: "Share with the Lord's people who are in need. Practice hospitality." (Romans 12:13) The Apostle Peter adds the warning that when we do so, it should be "without grumbling." (1 Peter 4:9) One of the qualities Paul lists for overseers is that they be "hospitable." (1 Timothy 3:2) Again, in writing to Titus, Paul puts first on a list of qualifications for overseers that they be hospitable. Such injunctions are not just for the "family." Christians, the writer to the Hebrews says, must not "forget to show hospitality to strangers, for by doing so some people have shown hospitality to angels without knowing it." (Hebrews 13:2) Think back to Abraham and the "three men" from God.

The concept of loving and welcoming strangers is a pivotal message of the New Testament. Beyond the Gospels, we learn about the central role hospitality played in the early days of Christianity. The young church regularly met in homes for times of worship. Because of this, the common meal became an important expression of hospitality that flourished in the multiracial society in which the early church was immersed.

In the fourth and fifth centuries, leaders like Jerome, John Chrysostom, Benedict of Nursia, and Lactantius kept the tradition and language of hospitality vibrant. However, by the medieval period, hospitality had become associated with entertainment and the personal advantage people could gain through it. Pohl writes, "In the diversity of institutions, the loss of the worshiping community as a significant site for hospitality and the differentiation of care among recipients, the socially transformative potential of hospitality was lost."[2]

With the Protestant Reformation of the 16th century came a reassertion of the importance of hospitality, perhaps driven in part by the upheaval in the social structures of Europe during the time. In the 18th century, John Wesley demanded a social understanding of the Gospel, and the Methodist movement he led reflected this articulation of social holiness. This social motivation was also prompted by an imminent millennial hope.[3]

Wesley clearly grasped the theological and moral significance of hospitality, but he didn't name it. Such semantic difficulty continues to perplex the contemporary church. Christians—Salvationists included— need to name the tradition of hospitality and see it as a means of understanding their social responsibility within the realms of theological, historical, and moral reflection. Naming hospitality as significant, even essential, to our work moves it beyond "duty" or "social services." Hospitality becomes a way of life for individuals and communities to express welcome as an outgrowth of their identity as a Christian body.

Pohl puts it this way: "... reclaiming hospitality is an attempt to bring back the relational dimension to social service, and to highlight concerns for empowerment and partnership for those who need assistance."[4] Any Christian movement that takes seriously the Apostle Paul's exhortation to "welcome one another" (Romans 15:7) can benefit from viewing this welcome through the lens of hospitality.

Chapter 3
A Holistic History

How have we as a Salvation Army practiced hospitality—making room for others—throughout our history? I believe that the greatest challenge facing the contemporary Army is implementing a historically informed social ethic. So, before I initiated change in the housing ministry in our corps in Arlington, Texas, I set out to examine the historical and theological foundations of The Salvation Army from its inception—and even before. What I uncovered was our holistic roots.[5]

In July 1865 in London's East End, an opportunity presented itself to Rev. William Booth to preach a series of revival meetings. Booth's heart ached for the people of this area.

> In every direction were multitudes totally ignorant of [the] gospel, and given up to all kinds of wickedness. … A voice seemed to sound in my ears, 'Why go … anywhere else, to find souls that need the Gospel? Here they are, tens of thousands at your very door. Preach to them, the unsearchable riches of Christ. I will help you—your need shall be supplied.'[6]

As in Booth's hometown of Nottingham, the negative effects of the Industrial Revolution had crippled the people of the East End. The industrialized urban areas of England fostered poverty, putting the lower classes into what Booth later called "the submerged tenth."[7] Between these people and the churches of the day a great wall gradually grew up.[8]

Philip Needham notes:

> As the lower classes became more and more estranged from the Church,
> an intense contradiction became apparent—a contradiction between the
> message of God's acceptance of all men through Christ and the obvious
> middle- and upper-class self-interest of those who espoused that
> message.[9]

When William Booth and his wife, Catherine, founded the East London
Christian Revival Society, their prime motivation was to preach the
Gospel to the East End people who were being neglected by the
churches. The Revival Society eventually became The Christian Mission;
the purpose of both was strictly evangelistic. The Booths established
"Preaching Stations," not churches. Their idea was that converts would
be channeled into the life of existing churches.

The Booths had no intention, initially, of starting a separate denomination.
William describes why their plans changed.

> My first idea was simply to get people saved, and send them to churches.
> This proved at the outset impracticable. 1st. [The converts] would not go
> when sent. 2nd. They were not wanted. And 3rd. We wanted some of them
> at least ourselves, to help us in the business of saving others. We were thus
> driven to providing for the converts ourselves.[10]

The Christian Mission grew to include 75 preaching stations and
120 evangelists. Then, in 1878, the Mission changed its name to The
Salvation Army and began to use military imagery to describe its
participants and practices. Within eight years of the name change, the
Army exploded to include 1,749 corps and 4,129 officers.[11] And Booth's
theology began to change. He was thinking more broadly about his
goals: his Army was still in the business of saving souls, but he also
believed that as an institution, the Army was sanctified, or set apart, to
bring about the Kingdom of God on Earth.[12]

But the Booths were also practical. They soon recognized that they could not possibly work in the midst of people who were struggling with poverty and social oppression for long with a singular focus on "souls," without recognizing that social and physical problems needed salvation too.[13]

Between 1878 and 1886, the Army grew to include 233 percent more corps and 344 percent more officers.[14] Scholar Ann Woodall points out that the ministry there became more effective and incarnational through such outreach programs as the "slum sisters," who lived among the poorest of the poor in order to reach them with the Gospel.[15]

Beginning in December 1883, the Army in Australia established and sustained a recovery home for released prisoners.[16]

Between 1884 and 1885, because of insights gained from a new rescue home for prostitutes, the Army launched an assault on sexual trafficking. This crusade highlighted the existence of a white slave trade in England, and with the help of investigative reporter W.T. Stead, the Salvation Army exposed the underground operation and forced the hand of Parliament to raise the age of consent from 13 to 16.[17]

In her book *Booth's Boots: Social Service Beginnings in The Salvation Army,* Major Jenty Fairbank discusses the Salvation Army's first forays into social work, including work with pregnant women, alcoholics, juvenile delinquents, and prisoners as well as establishment of anti-suicide, reconciliation, and shelter ministries. Many of these efforts began before 1890.[18]

Historian Pamela J. Walker observes that between 1884 and 1890, the programs that the Army set up were designed to relieve the distress of people living in poverty. She also notes that the Army's purpose was to "exert a religious influence on those believed too burdened to seek it on their own." From 1884 on, Walker writes, "The Salvation Army slowly shaped a dual mission ..."[19]

This idea developed gradually. By 1889, William Booth articulated it in his famous article, "Salvation for Both Worlds."[20] It was a statement of mature theological expression that understood both the social and spiritual aspects of the Christian message. Booth recognized that holistic ministry, which sought salvation of body and soul, was necessary.

> I had two gospels of deliverance to preach—one for each world [temporal or eternal], or rather, one gospel which applied alike to both. I saw that when the Bible said, 'He that believeth shall be saved,' it meant not only saved from the miseries of the future world, but from the miseries of this [world] also.[21]

It was Booth, as part of his millennial understanding, who in 1890 first distinguished the "Social Wing" by making it an office with its own officers and commissioner, with himself as the autocratic link between that wing and others within the Army.[22]

The Social Wing's objective was to implement the "scheme" Booth described in *In Darkest England and the Way Out*. In this book, the Army Founder explicitly supported and institutionally expanded on the social ministries that had been operating since 1884.[23]

Underlying Booth's grand "Darkest England" plan was a belief that the indwelling power of the Holy Spirit could bring about change in the whole world. He had been influenced by the American holiness movement, which placed a new emphasis on the role of the Holy Spirit in the process of both salvation and sanctification.[24] For Booth, this meant that his Army would not just be about saving souls but saving social systems as well. His urgency in going about this dual mission was to bring about the millennial reign of Christ before His second coming.[25] If this reign could not come about until the world and its social systems were all Christianized, Booth reasoned, then Christians had an urgent mission, an ethical responsibility, to make that happen.

Booth was always looking toward "the last things." But the fact that he was did not mean that the plight of people around him diminished in focus. On the contrary, the "end" for him broke into the present as a guide to ethical action.

How Christians view God's Kingdom in society affects how they are active in the world. By 1890, Booth's millennialism and social ethic were fully developed. They formed the foundation of the holistic ministry that The Salvation Army embodied. In the midst of this development, Booth never lost his zeal for souls. In his most explicit writing on eschatology, "The Millenium [sic]; or, The Ultimate Triumph of Salvation Army Principles," Booth illustrates how his personal eschatology fit within his universal eschatology.

> The most effective methods of advancing the happiness of mankind, and bringing in the Millenial [sic] reign, must be the rule of God in the hearts and lives of men, and the spread of the principles of righteousness and love.[26]

The particular way that The Salvation Army promoted the "principles of righteousness and love" was its distinctive approach to social ethics. When these principles were blended with millennialism, a dynamic holistic missiology emerged. William Booth's ethical perspective is, therefore, an expression of his eschatology, or what I call his eschatological ethic.[27] This ethic recognizes that the mission of the Kingdom is the mission for God's people now. In "Salvation for Both Worlds," Booth elaborates on the ethic's incarnational quality:

> Christ is the deliverer for time as truly as for eternity. He is the Joshua who leads men in our own day out of the wilderness into the Promised Land, as His forerunner did the Children of Israel thousands of years ago. He is the messiah who brings glad tidings! He is come to open the prison doors. He is come to set men free from their bonds. He is indeed the Saviour of the world![28]

Did William Booth's theological foundation accompany The Salvation Army after his death? That is hard to ascertain. The perceptive historian of Salvation Army history, Edward H. McKinley, suggests that the rank and file workers of The Salvation Army

> ... were little concerned with theories of social justice, they knew only that their Heavenly Commander had ordered His soldiers to take in strangers, visit the sick and imprisoned, and offer drink to the thirsty and food to the hungry. They also knew that there were souls dying all around and that the first step in saving some of them was to lift them up so they could hear that such a thing as salvation existed.[29]

What was impressed upon The Salvation Army by William Booth was a holistic theology that was developed by his own eschatological vision and the way he felt God was using his Army in that process.

The Salvation Army became involved with housing ministries very early in its history: two of the earliest were Australia's "Prison Gate" Home, founded in 1883, and the Rescue Home, born in London in 1884, overseen by William and Catherine Booth's daughter-in-law, Florence Booth. This home was a residential facility for the recovery of prostituted women.[30]

For the purposes of my project, which would involve our transitional housing program in Arlington, I set out to look at similar ministries in the United States.

The first rescue home, serving unwed mothers and women escaping prostitution, was established in Brooklyn just six years after the Salvation Army "invaded" the United States. The front page of the 1886 *War Cry* declared in a headline: "Rescue Home for Fallen and Homeless Girls: The Salvation Army to the Rescue."[31]

Then, in 1897, Frederick Booth-Tucker, national commander, initiated the Men's Social Wing, with an ambitious goal of having a "salvage brigade" in every American city with a population larger than 10,000. The brigade combined job training and ministry to the homeless; those being served through the early housing programs of the brigade were trained to work through reselling of goods donated to The Salvation Army.[32]

By the turn of the century, the Army had two administrative weapons for fighting homelessness: the Men's Social Wing and the Women's Social Service Department. Both programs expanded and thrived over the next several decades.

Under the leadership of Colonel Richard E. Holz, the Men's Social Wing, beginning in 1899, established Industrial Homes for Men.[33] These homes, commonly called "The Dusties," gave men in the programs shelter and an opportunity to work through rehabilitation. The Industrial Homes became Men's Social Service Centers in the 1920s, when the Social Wing became the Men's Social Service Department. The service centers took on their current name, Adult Rehabilitation Centers, in 1977. Today, that ministry, which sometimes has women as well as men as beneficiaries, is active throughout the U.S.

The Women's Social Service Department and its rescue homes also became effective and in 1920 took on a new name, The Salvation Army Home and

Hospital.[34] This program received high acclaim for its effectiveness in leading unwed mothers to stable living. A Rockefeller study of 1924 noted: "These homes collectively [were] without question the Army's most successful contribution to the social field."[35]

Waves of social change in the second half of the 20th century led to the evaporation of this effort. The introduction of birth control pills in the 1960s and the legalization of abortion in the 70s decreased the need for such services. In a thoughtful study, Beatrice Combs notes that liability was a further issue: "loss of charitable immunity, an increasingly litigious society, and exorbitant cost of liability insurance and of hospital costs in the wake of Medicaid combined to make The Salvation Army's delivering of health care prohibitive."[36] By 1975, the modern descendant of the Rescue Home—the Home and Hospital—no longer existed.

But The Salvation Army still had a strong theological motivation to serve those entrapped by the forces of society. So it found new ways to serve families in local communities. In the 1950s, the transient lodge emerged as a place for homeless people to stay as they made their way from town to town. When society changed so that the traveling homeless person was no longer a phenomenon in the United States, the Army adapted, opening shelters for local homeless people. Eventually this ministry changed again; the shelters became either emergency or transitional shelters.

Emergency shelters are specifically established for people in need of short-term housing. Transitional shelters exist as a point between short-term emergency shelter and independent housing. Throughout the world, The Salvation Army operates more than 4,000 residential shelters with the potential of housing more than 107,000 people.[37]

As society has changed, other models have been developed for housing ministry. For instance, Gwinnett County, Georgia, where I began serving in 2012, operates a "housing first" or "scattered site" model that does not utilize the capital resources needed for a shelter. Instead, households in this program stay in homes provided by the Army. The statistics for residential shelters don't include people using these new programs. The program in Gwinnett, for example, provides more than 23,000 nights of shelter each year.

Chapter 4
Bridging the Social *vs.* Spiritual Divide

Commissioner Frank Smith, the first leader of the Social Wing, described the unique mission of The Salvation Army in Victorian society.

> … the fact is, deny it who can, the churches are wedded to the wealthy world. Let us of The Salvation Army, from this day forth, wed ourselves to the fate and fortunes of the so-called dangerous classes. Let us go down to our bride in the Boweries of our cities. God approves of this union.[38]

In the early Salvationists' zeal for reaching people who needed temporal as well as spiritual help, balance was important. The way in which people understood that balance between what is social and what is spiritual was an issue in the beginning of the Army and is still an issue today.

Brigadier Fred Cox, personal secretary to William Booth, recalled how Booth would often respond to questions about this dilemma.

> He believed in keeping religion first. People used to say to him in the early days, 'You know, General, we can do with your social operations, but we can't do with your religion; we don't want it.' The General would say—'If you want my Social Work, you have got to have my Religion; they are joined together like Siamese twins; to divide them is to slay them!'[39]

Harmonizing these two aspects of Salvation Army ministry can be a challenge for any Salvationist. In 1966 Philip Needham described the Army as "schizophrenic."[40] On the other hand, General Frederick Coutts described the idealized mutual existence of social and spiritual ministries as a marriage.[41] Coutts also found a unique analogy that helped move the Army away from separating social and spiritual ministries.

> Every effort made by The Salvation Army is directed to helping man work out the complete salvation of his entire personality through the power of God. I therefore ask our many friends not to attempt to divide our activities into 'social' and 'religious.' These are false opposites. In effect, they are one—two sides of the same sheet of paper, two conjoined aspects of the one and indivisible work of grace.[42]

The individual Salvationist today understands all of the Army's social activities as based in the Christian message. But often, the public as well as Salvationists themselves have continued to separate the Army's ministries into "social" and "spiritual." Even scholars within The Salvation Army have found it difficult to make the Army's social service ministries fit into a theological system. This dilemma is apparent in the title of the important work, *Creed and Deed: Toward a Christian Theology of Social Work in The Salvation Army*,[43] edited by a key thinker in Salvation Army studies, Commissioner John D. Waldron.

The papers offered in *Creed and Deed* begin with what I believe is a flawed premise: that "social services" is (or should be) the overarching paradigm of Salvation Army social ministry.[44] This paradigm is inadequate because it fails to place The Salvation Army within the larger narrative of Christian social action. Identifying "social services" as separate from other aspects of The Salvation Army can create an impersonal atmosphere for those we serve and a "professional" distinction for those doing the serving.[45]

In practice, this separation can mean that when soldiers of a corps who faithfully attend Sunday holiness meetings encounter a person in need of "temporal" salvation,[46] they might say, "You'll have to come back on Monday during business hours." While it's true that the person may need professional case management and thorough analysis of the situation, holistic hospitality should call Salvationists to a more humanizing task of connecting to people—beyond a referral. Divorcing the so-called "spiritual work" from "social work" can be an unhealthy pattern and paradigm.

Has the insufficient paradigm of "social services" meant that we as an Army have put too much emphasis on this split?

In my own setting in Arlington, I could easily see how that split often plays out: We had the "church," and we had the "shelter." I asked myself, *Could there be a better way to go about social ministry, one that would be consistent with Booth's holistic vision?*

Chapter 5

Our Hospitable Heritage

How can the Army be true to the legacy of William Booth's eschatological ethic and holistic approach to mission? Recent scholarship has rediscovered the paradigm and practice of hospitality as a way of approaching Christian social ethics. Just listen to some titles of recent books: *Making Room: Recovering Hospitality as a Christian Tradition* (Christine D. Pohl, 1999); *The Gift of Hospitality: In Church, in the Home, in All of Life* (Delia Touchton Halverson, 1999); *God's Welcome: Hospitality for a Gospel-Hungry World* (Amy G. Oden, 2008); and *Hospitality as Holiness: Christian Witness Amid Moral Diversity* (Luke Bretherton, 2010).

For The Salvation Army, employing the paradigm of hospitality is not a new thing. William Booth's personal ministry and theological development can be seen as a journey toward hospitality. At first, he was focused on offering personal redemption to groups that society neglected. Eventually, he saw the need for the Army to welcome the whole person.

Booth famously said that the cab-horse in London had three things: "A shelter for the night, food for its stomach, and work allotted to it by which it can eat its corn."[47] Those basic rights given to horses, Booth said, were being denied to the "submerged tenth" of the population.

In other words, those people were invisible to society. But Booth recognized them because, he believed, they were people for whom Jesus died. Booth saw within each person the possibility of deliverance from sin and social evil because, in his theology, he understood that salvation was available for each person.

Booth *recognized* the people that Victorian society did not. *In Darkest England* was his effort to transport the theme of social redemption to the forefront of people's thinking. Today, that power of *recognition* is a key theme in the tradition of hospitality.[48]

Possibly drawing on the language of Matthew 25, Booth later in the book stresses the power of dignity and respect:

> But we who call ourselves by the name of Christ are not worthy to profess to be His disciples until we have set an open door before the least and worst of these who are now apparently imprisoned for life in a horrible dungeon of misery and despair.[49]

The Booths and John Wesley recognized that God's *prevenient grace* was at work in people's lives, and this understanding dramatically transformed their outlook on social ethics. Catherine Booth, speaking about visitation to people in their homes, said:

> They need to be brought into contact with a living Christ … they want to see and handle the words of life in a living form. Christianity must come to them embodied in men and women, who are not ashamed to 'eat with publicans and sinners.'[50]

Catherine also recognized the significance of seeing Jesus in every stranger: "Oh, for grace to see Him where He is to be seen, for verily, flesh and blood doth not reveal this unto us! Well … I keep seeing Him risen again in the forms of drunkards and ruffians of all descriptions."[51]

Bramwell Booth expressed his own passion for those the fledgling Army had invited in:

When I see the poor, shivering creatures gathered in the warmth and comfort of our Shelters, and the famished ones in the Food Depots, and the lost and lonely in the bright hopefulness of the Women's and Children's Homes, and the prisoners—set in happy families in our Harbours of Refuge, my heart sings for joy, and I say, *Is this not the Christ come again?*[52]

William recognized the importance of Jesus' teaching on "who is my neighbor?" (Luke 10:29–37) as he urged soldiers "to observe continually the sacrament of the Good Samaritan."[53]

Then, of course, there is the famous conversation, recorded in *Echoes and Memories,* that Bramwell Booth had with his father when the two were crossing the Thames River on London Bridge and William saw men sleeping under the arches at nightfall. Bramwell was aware that the men were homeless, but William was outraged by what he saw and said to his son (Bramwell's responses in italics):

'Go and do something! We must do something.' *'What can we do?'* 'Get them a shelter!' *'That will cost money.'* 'Well, that is your affair! Something must be done. Get hold of a warehouse and warm it, and find something to cover them. But mind, Bramwell, no coddling!'[54]

Despite Booth's admonition against coddling, it's obvious that for him, hospitality was an imperative.

The early Salvation Army presents the contemporary Army and the Christian church in general with a prophetic social ethic that has at its core an implicit form of hospitality. It is this legacy of hospitality and holistic ministry that could serve as the lens through which the contemporary Army looks to the future.

In recent times, the first challenge to view our ministries through this lens came from Miroslav Volf, who gave a keynote lecture to the Salvation

Army's International Theology and Ethics Symposium in 2001. Volf said that in caring for others, "The exclusive pursuit of justice will not do. We need more than justice, not less. We need grace."[54] Then he explained that hospitality is a form of grace.

> Hospitality has at its background some need of the person to whom we are hospitable (food, shelter, human touch, love, etc.) If we don't offer hospitality, we do the person no wrong; if we do offer it, we give something more than the person had a claim upon.[55]

Volf connected the welcome of hospitality to the life of the Economic Trinity (which speaks of each person of the Godhead having different roles in relationship to the world).

> We don't know why the world was created; we just know that this divine love sought a place to 'spill itself over.' ... Part and parcel of the economic Trinity is not only creating a world in an incredible act of generosity and sustaining it in an act of hospitality, but also engaging the world in love to restore it to a communion it once had with God, a communion that has now been ravaged by sin and death.[56]

For the past 150 years, the Army has arguably had the most consistent social witness. But theological reflection has often been a secondary concern for a pragmatic Salvation Army, which means that we don't have an explicit theological foundation for our practices. I believe it is important for us to acknowledge, name, and refocus our social witness as "hospitality." If we do, our work will be firmly rooted in the theological history of the Church. We can also be assured that our social ministries are grounded in the theology of hospitality and in the legacy of our Founders.

Chapter 6
Hospitality in Arlington, Texas

When my wife and I were serving in our fifth year as corps officers of the Arlington Corps, we began to look at how the paradigm of hospitality might be applied in the setting of the Family Life Center (FLC), the corps' housing ministry.

Arlington is a relatively young corps. An outpost[58] was established there in 1985, and it became a corps in 1989. Three years after its opening, the corps moved from a small rental space in a medical office building to a 38,000–square–foot building that included a 12,500–square–foot family shelter. The building went up, but the immense capacity for holistic mission was not realized. To complicate matters, the tenure of corps officers had been very brief. From 1989 to 2007, the average length of appointment was 1.66 years. The family shelter, which needed efficient records for government contracts, effectively became separated from the corps.

My own personal affinity was toward the corps. As a sixth–generation officer in The Salvation Army, most of my life as a Salvationist has been spent in various corps congregations.[59] But as the corps officer, I was the steward[60] of the family shelter and all the constituencies who played a part in the Arlington ministries: the advisors, the corps members, paid staff and volunteers, and the people we served. In my first few years as a corps officer, I felt challenged by the multiple hats I had to wear in leading each of these groups. While each was generally aware that the others existed, they did not necessarily communicate among themselves.

As the corps officer, I communicated with each of the groups, but I had never spoken to all four groups at one time.

So I set out to remedy this situation. The essence of the idea would be to allow the people who identify themselves as a part of The Salvation Army to be united in mission and visioning—around the idea of hospitality—for the future of missional activity. I decided to focus my attention on one specific program, the housing ministry, because I realized that if I tried to implement a shift for every program of the corps, it would be extremely difficult to measure whether the changes had made a difference.

Representatives from Four Groups

The first of the four groups to be represented was the corps congregation, which I defined as people who understand and claim The Salvation Army as their spiritual home—soldiers, adherents, and people who attend but haven't made a commitment to membership.

Often in The Salvation Army there have been efforts to include the voices of the soldiery, but allowing them to speak without representation from the corps congregation at large, in my view, lessens the impact of Salvation Army mission because key voices go unheard. For the purposes of my project, I believed that including all the voices from the congregation had the potential to impact and refresh Salvation Army ministries in Arlington. In a larger sense, this inclusion prophetically insists to the larger Salvation Army that a greater effort must be made to define those who make up our congregations.

The second group to be invited was the advisors. An advisory organization[61] is defined by The Salvation Army internationally as "a group of influential citizens who, believing in the Army's programme [sic] of spiritual, moral, and physical rehabilitation and amelioration, assist in promoting and supporting Army projects."[62] While their decisions and recommendations are generally followed, the command structure of The Salvation Army delegates final authority to the ecclesial leadership of officers.

The Salvation Army Arlington Advisory Council comes under the leadership of the DFW–Metroplex Advisory Board, which is based in Dallas. The advisory council's tasks are facilitating programs and raising support. At the time we served in Arlington, of the $1.6 million budget for the corps, only $40,000, or 2.5 percent, of the annual budget came in through Sunday offerings from the congregation. It was the council's responsibility to secure the rest of the funds to sustain the corps' mission.

A third group involved in the project was the staff. More than 20 employees, both full- and part-time, worked in the day-to-day operations of the corps. At the time we served in Arlington, the housing ministries had three full-time and six part-time staff members. Beyond the shelter, a variety of employees were active, either as program or support staff, in the delivery of Salvation Army programs. One of the challenges the staff faced is that though they had interaction with the guests of the shelter and other recipients of program services, they were generally unconnected to the congregation and the advisory council. It was particularly challenging for staff, who work during weekday office hours, to have a grasp of the ecclesiological foundation for the Salvation Army's ministry.

The last group involved in the Salvation Army's ministry in Arlington were the individuals who benefited from programs, especially those residing in the Family Life Center (FLC), the corps' transitional shelter for families. In my first five years as a Salvation Army officer, I had heard these friends referred to as clients, residents, or beneficiaries. I was not very supportive of these titles, so I found it helpful to change the language. In the winter of 2010, I began referring to participants in our housing programs as *guests*.

Few shelters in the area offer private spaces where families can stay together. Instead, most shelters separate family members by gender and move older children to dorms with homeless adult strangers. This leaves already vulnerable children even more at risk. The Family Life Center is a place where a homeless family—typically, two adults and three children—live and eat together in apartments with private bedrooms and bathrooms as they make the transition from homelessness to permanent housing.[63]

Through the FLC, the Salvation Army of Arlington uplifts families in a safe, supportive environment that promotes education, stability, and wholeness. It provides a 24–week transitional self–sufficiency program. When families enter the program, they are often overwhelmed by frustration, stress, hopelessness, anger, and confusion. These needs are addressed first, and then staff work on the underlying issues that led to the family's homelessness, all with a view to breaking the cycle of poverty.

How Do the Groups Interact?

A daunting aspect of the project is that all four of these groups needed to have critical buy–in of my proposal for renewal of the housing ministries of the Arlington Salvation Army. Another personal challenge was to avoid the tendency in my own thinking to separate the Army's activity and my leadership among these groups. Before I started, I took a look at what kinds of interactions the groups typically have with one another.

The congregation interacted with some guests from the shelter who participated in the corps' activities. Often, the people of the congregation connected with the families as a way of expressing their faith. The congregation had little involvement with the advisory council, the only exception being when the corps hosted an Advisory Council Sunday. On that occasion, members of the congregation would surround council members and pray for them, and council members would be recognized for their service.

The staff members had an awareness of the other three groups because their job was to facilitate the environment in which the others operated. But most staff members had never been a part of any other segment of Salvation Army ministries. The group the staff interacted with most were the guests of the shelter. The guests interacted daily with cooks, security monitors, and support staff. But the staff, with the exception of the few who are also members of the congregation, had little involvement with the congregation because they were typically not in the building at the same time.

Some guests interacted with members of the congregation, but most had only a cursory understanding that The Salvation Army in Arlington had a functioning congregation. However, through the years of the ministry of the Family Life Center, which opened in 1992, a few families continued to be active in the congregation after they had completed the program.

The advisory council had little interaction with the shelter guests except that twice a year, the council heard testimonies from guests. While this was always a highlight on the council agenda, guests and council members essentially remained unknown to one another.

Creating a Task Force

I designed the project to have four phases. First, I would set up and meet with a task force to design a curriculum for what I at first called the "educational session." Second, people from all the corps' constituencies would be invited to the educational session, planned to run three hours and help participants to connect the biblical, historical, and theological concepts presented in the earlier chapters of this book to the idea of hospitality. In that session, the participants would brainstorm and finally distill two ideas that could refresh the theological praxis of the housing ministry. Third, the changes that emerged from this session would be implemented in the shelter. Fourth, I would reflect on and evaluate the project.

In forming a task force, I had to consider how a nucleus of three people might help me develop, design, and shape the educational session. I knew that these three people could not represent the broad perspectives of each group, but I sought out individuals who brought a representative knowledge of their own cluster of Salvation Army ministry. In a spirit of sensitivity regarding the way the educational session could affect guests, I elected not to include a guest of the shelter as part of the task force. But as part of the educational session, a dialogue period would allow ample time for our guests to share their stories and perspectives on the effectiveness of our housing ministry.[64]

One staff member included on the task force was our minister of hospitality, Martin J.,[65] who was in charge of the Family Life Center. The previous job title for the position had been Family Life Center manager. During our tenure as corps officers, my wife and I had worked with two such managers. Both experiences led us to believe that an explicit connection needed to be made between the guests of the shelter and the corps congregation. This goal required several months of administrative change that would allow the job description to be altered. All the responsibilities remained the same through the transition; what changed were a few updated clauses and, most obviously, the title, minister of hospitality. Under the heading of "essential functions" in the job description, we added that the person "facilitates the involvement of Soldiers and Adherents from the corps' congregation within the ministry of the Family Life Center." Also, the job description was changed to require that the minister of hospitality attend worship services "with the intention of enabling the local corps congregation's understanding of the Salvation Army's housing ministries" and participate in the regular activities of the corps congregation. The minister of hospitality would also have "the ability to present the biblical and theological basis for the Salvation Army's housing ministries."

When Martin was hired in 2011, he understood that his job title was biblically and theologically rooted; however, he was not fully aware of my plans to use hospitality as a concept in the Family Life Center. Martin, an ordained minister with a bachelor's degree in practical ministry, had previously worked for The Salvation Army in another Texas city. In 10 years of experience in other homeless programs, he had felt his hands were often tied and that he couldn't holistically serve the people to whom he was called. As a member of the task force, Martin would represent his fellow employees as well as the guests of the shelter.

Cynthia A. represented the congregation on the task force. The child of officer parents, Cynthia grew up knowing The Salvation Army as her church. She and her first husband had served as officers for a couple of years in the Carolinas Division of the Army. After divorce and remarriage, Cynthia and her three kids became part of our congregation. An employee of the Army's Adult Rehabilitation Center in Dallas, she was the most active member of the congregation at the time the task force was selected. She served as a leader of the women's ministry program and secretary for the corps council, and she took on behind-the-scenes roles for Sunday worship. She also empowered her children to be active participants in every possible youth program. Her involvement as well as her knowledge of Salvation Army culture and history would enable her to be a helpful member of the task force.

Dixon H., chair of our advisory council, was selected to represent this constituency. He was a former Arlington city council member and mayor pro-tem of the city. A successful businessperson, he was well known throughout Tarrant County. He was also a second-generation advisory organization member; both his parents had served on advisory organizations in the area. His knowledge of The Salvation Army would bring a community development perspective to the task force. When my wife and I arrived in Arlington, the advisory council had just four active members. Dixon came onto the council midway through our first year, began chairing the council in his second year, and helped to bring more members onto the council and make it a more definite influence in Arlington. He and his family attended

Trinity United Methodist Church, an active missional partner of the Arlington Corps.

A date was set for the first meeting of the task force. It was time for the real work to begin.

Chapter 7

The Task Force Digs In

The task force members—Martin, minister of hospitality at the Family Life Center; Cynthia, an active soldier and leader in the congregation; Dixon, chair of the advisory council, and I—were to meet on a Saturday morning three weeks before the planned educational session. In inviting each of them, I had informed them that this project was part of my doctoral work at Southern Methodist University. And I had given them homework; I asked them to read my own work on the biblical, theological, and theoretical foundations I had outlined for the project (which appear in Chapters 2–4 of this book), as well as one of the sermons I had delivered on hospitality (Chapter 1).

As the day approached, I admit I felt a bit of anxiety about whether these three people—and later, the larger group of the educational session— would be able to work together. I knew they were all on the same page with our mission statement, but we had never had an opportunity to "live" that experience together. As an officer, I was used to wearing multiple hats, and this would be my first attempt to engender a sense of unity in mission behind my leadership.

Well, Saturday morning did come. After opening in prayer, I spent some time exploring the members' personal narratives. I explained why I thought each was an ideal person for the task force and how each one had contributed to the success of the Arlington Corps. This was a good opportunity for me to be an encourager, and it served to introduce members of the task force to one another.

Next, I began to review my prospectus, which I had given to the task force members. Immediately, Dixon took out his copy, which I could see was underlined and notated. At his cue, Martin and Cynthia did the same. As soon as I said, "Do you follow me here?" it was as if the starting gate at a horse race had opened as the people around table galloped to give their opinions.

Martin wanted to implement some of the ideas right then in the Family Life Center (FLC). Then he said that in another Salvation Army unit where he had worked, such a dramatic change couldn't possibly have happened. When I essentially said that I couldn't speak for that other unit, he said, "Captain, don't get me wrong. The Salvation Army [there] was the most Christian social service environment I have ever worked for. But it was just that—social services. They had a Christian atmosphere, but there was a clear line between social services and ministry."[66]

Dixon immediately wanted the refocusing on hospitality to be a national program that would be implemented in every corps. That, of course, had been my own first impulse, and I was tempted to talk more about how the Army can be true to its holistic mission, one of my favorite topics. But I didn't do that. I pointed out to Dixon a place in my prospectus (an academic document guiding this project) under the heading, "what I will not do," where I said that I would not attempt to change the Salvation Army's approach to housing ministries but would focus solely on the Army's service in Arlington.

Cynthia said she thought the larger Army would be open to change but would want to see a program working first. She thought the project was a good idea because the people of the corps frequently hear others say, "I didn't know The Salvation Army is a church." She also said that she saw a similarity between what the project would be trying to do and the change that had happened when the Salvation Army Thrift

Stores became Family Stores. Nods of affirmation came from the others, including me.

When we began to talk about the biblical, theological, and theoretical material, Dixon was the most vocal. At one point, he said, "When I read what you quoted about Booth telling his son to 'do something' about homelessness, I thought, *Boy, we really have been doing something.*"

Dixon's comment helped to clarify for Martin and Cynthia that as advisory council chair, he understood the Army's activity to be connected to its church heritage. His comment showed that he was including himself as part of that Christian action.

Then Dixon made a point that shed new light for me. "The Army can do this because it is an army and not The Salvation Church. We can do more because we have an efficient structure, and we are not having to make people happy by being a church in the traditional sense." While I agreed, I was sensitive to Cynthia's just-acknowledged desire for The Salvation Army to be known as a church. I realized that this tension would need to be managed as we walked through the task force meeting and the project as a whole.

When I talked through what is meant by Christian hospitality and how that can serve as a guiding vision for renewing the shelter's ministry, I felt confident that the group understood the big idea of where we were going.

Then we discussed the goals of the educational session: to help people learn about hospitality as a guiding paradigm and to develop at least two ideas to implement in our Family Life Center. I explained that there would be an educational session for youth of the shelter as well.

I started to lay out the proposed schedule for the session and how we would begin with introductions. Cynthia raised her hand and said, "This might not be the right time for this question, but how is the room going to be set up?" I didn't have a good answer. I had thought we would just set up chairs facing the screen, so people could see my PowerPoint.

Cynthia made the point that she would want a table so she could write during the meeting. So I drew a layout for the room with tables placed horizontally facing the screen.

Dixon interjected, "The problem with that, Andy, is that some people will be at the front and others at the back. It will be too easy for people to become disengaged. If the focus is to share ideas … and come to some concrete decisions, there has to be commonality."

I admitted that I hadn't given the layout of the room much thought. But the task force members thought it very important. So we decided to make the room into a U shape—with the presenter in the center—so the participants would be able to engage one another. The task force was beginning to function exactly as I hoped it would. Much of our work became a co-learning process.

Martin offered another practical idea: provide snacks and coffee. Cynthia suggested that each participant have a notepad; Dixon added that we should place a placard before each person with their name on them, as the advisory council did. Cynthia said, "Oh, that would make it feel like it is an important event." We accepted all the suggestions.

Then I raised the topic of how to introduce everyone to each other. I asked, "How do we do that without separating ourselves into groups?" I had a specific concern about how to respect the shelter guests. We discussed in detail whether we should even introduce ourselves beyond our names. But we ultimately came to the conclusion that it would be better to have knowledge of the people so that we could understand the perspective each brought.

Regarding the challenge of identifying shelter guests, the task force decided to have Martin meet with guests who could participate; he would decide if their identification as guests of the FLC would affect them negatively in any way. This also would give Martin the chance to let the guests know that this would not be the time to complain about small details, but that we *would* be looking for their honest responses.

I asked the task force whether introductions should be done in small groups (four people) or with the group as a whole. Dixon said that there would be significant diversity in the room, and he did not want to miss hearing how people had come to participate in the Arlington Salvation Army.

Then I asked whether I should mention that the session was a part of a degree program for my doctorate of ministry.

Martin instantly responded: "Absolutely." Dixon said it should be mentioned but in the advertising for the event. He joked, "Don't put on the flyer, 'Come help Captain Andy get his doctorate.' " Cynthia thought it could be slid into the discussion and that it would be a point of pride for the congregation. I told them how the project had evolved, from taking a class on hospitality for social ethics with Dr. Christine Pohl at Asbury Theological Seminary to writing papers and articles and speaking at a social service conference on the theme. The task force felt that I could share these things, using self-deprecating humor, and mention that the project is a significant portion of my degree work at SMU.

Then the task force took on the problem of the title I had given our upcoming larger meeting: educational session. They thought it unappealing and even possibly counterproductive. I admit I had thought of the session partially as teaching. But the task force members said that while it was important to share information, what was more important was that real action take place in the Family Life Center. Dixon put it in a nutshell.

"I know what you mean, Andy, but calling this an educational session sounds like you are going to sit down and tell people something, which misses the point of what you are really trying to accomplish. Yes, we want them to learn something, but we want their perspective in light of what they have learned."

So we started to think about how the title of the session could fit its function. Someone suggested it was like a Salvation Army "think tank." But that term seemed too political. Dixon summarized the outline of the session. "Basically, we have three big ideas: where we are, where we are going, and how we get there."

While we were wrestling, Cynthia came up with a description that seemed to fit the goal: "thinking and acting on the mission of the Family Life Center." We dissected that for a while. The way the word "mission" was being thrown around the task force gave me concern. In The Salvation Army, it's easy to talk about our mission as a strategic battlefield perspective. It seems as if we make plans for God and then call it a mission. I referred the task force to a statement I had made in my prospectus that identified missional thinking as an ecclesiological perspective that places a heavy emphasis on the way the church is sent to be a *part* of God's mission to redeem the world. Rowan Williams famously said, "It is not the church of God that has a mission. It's the God of mission that has a church."[67]

We felt good about the description then being "thinking, acting, and understanding the mission God has for the Salvation Army's Family Life Center." This focus was helpful for our work group and provided a foundation for the discussion that followed.

Cynthia proposed that the educational session be called "Bridging the Gap." I welcomed her idea but explained that saying there is a gap starts with a negative presupposition. I was not sure that our shelter had a problem that could be identified as a gap. Instead, I thought, we were trying to refresh and renew the theological praxis of this ministry.

I brought up the concept of using hospitality in the name of the event. While each member of the task force had a grasp on the value of the word and the theological concept as a way of bringing about renewal, they all thought that the word would be more valuable after the session. "If people see an advertisement for a 'hospitality forum,' they might be confused, thinking this is a homemakers' session and be less inclined to attend," Dixon said.

Martin brought us back to the bridge metaphor. "I know we don't want to talk about a problem with gaps and other concerns, but what's wrong with a bridge? A bridge does not mean separation. It means getting somewhere. You can have a city that is connected by a bridge and it is still the same city. We are wanting people to be more connected, so we should have bridges all over the place."

The group seemed to respond to his insight. It became clear to me that my caution about not implying separation had likely been overstated. My conviction had almost disabled the group from thinking creatively about the process. Thankfully, Martin's winsome comments enabled us to think with a fresh mindset about the word "bridge." The group took his energy and ran with it. Eventually, we settled on the title, "Building a Bridge: Thinking, Acting, and Understanding God's Mission for the Salvation Army's Family Life Center."

Practical Considerations

The task force's next goal was to figure out how we should structure a tour of the center. We realized that giving a tour to 30 people could be a problem because of the difficulty of finding a way for everyone to hear, especially in tight spaces. I wondered aloud if we should break the group up.

The response was quick and strong: the task force thought that the group should stay together so that individuals from the four constituencies could have conversations throughout the tour. One challenge was that we would be entering the back door of the shelter and walking toward the front; then we would have to walk back through the entire building again. I suggested an idea that I wasn't sure would work because of the summer heat wave—walking through the parking lot toward the shelter entrance. Then we would walk up the long staircase leading to the entrance, which would give everyone the same experience as families entering the shelter for the first time. Cynthia added that we could ask participants to imagine what it would be like to be living in their cars, then stepping out and walking to the shelter doors. She wasn't concerned about the triple–digit weather; she thought walking in the heat would give us all a better sense of what a new family experiences when they come to the FLC.

When and How to Brainstorm

Next, we needed to discuss how to conduct the brainstorming session. I asked a series of questions: Should we brainstorm in small groups; if so, how should they be divided? Should we tell people in advance that we will be brainstorming? Or should we tell them after the opening segment, or at the end of the session? How many ideas would we consider? How would we form a consensus?

Cynthia started the discussion. "I think it would be good to let people know at the beginning because then they can take notes throughout the forum." Martin said, "Yeah, that makes sense." Dixon responded diplomatically:

I see what you are saying, Cynthia: the only challenge with having people write their ideas down is that they might miss the big picture. … We have some important things to say about the Army and how this can help us get where we need to be. … I think there is real power in letting the ideas and the tour settle in people's minds and then giving them a chance to have input through the brainstorming session.

There was pretty much no argument after that. Dixon had proposed a concept and really a methodical approach. So the basic flow of the educational session would be first to learn who we were and how we all constituted The Salvation Army; second, to present the Army's mission and history and a vision for what it could be; third, to experience the ministry through a tour and testimony; fourth, to create an environment for brainstorming ideas that could be implemented immediately.

The task force started to drift toward the big picture again. It was as if a light bulb had gone off in our thinking.

Cynthia expressed the excitement we felt. "We could use this same model for every program in the corps."

"Like I said at the beginning—and I know Andy wants us to keep focused on this project—I don't see why this shouldn't be implemented nationally," Dixon said.

Then we got back to the specifics of the brainstorming session. Would all 30 people shout ideas to a person who would write them down, or would we break into smaller groups? I proposed that we have people from each sector represented in each group so that everyone would be able to hear how a current shelter guest felt about the program.

Dixon led the way in this discussion; he felt that each group could get more done if they stayed together in their subgroups. Cynthia agreed. She felt that people would feel more "comfortable sharing ideas with people they know." I was unconvinced. Martin made a final comment that opened the door to my concession. "You know, Captain, the residents will probably come up with more ideas if they are together." I decided to accept the collective wisdom of the group.

The task force also set up the logistics of the brainstorming session. Every group would have 20 minutes to respond to questions in four areas: facility updates, the naming of services, programs, and interaction among the groups represented at the educational session. Each group would have a recorder who would write down every idea, then the group would select their top two ideas. The task force felt a couple of ideas would emerge as consistent areas for refreshing the theological praxis of the FLC. The group as a whole would then select and vote on two ideas that could be implemented two weeks after the session.

Who Should Be Invited?

Our final goal was to determine who should be invited to the session. The corps congregation was the largest group from which to draw participants. We agreed that we didn't want one group to dominate; however, we did want to have specific people attend. Cynthia suggested inviting one man who had been homeless and had spent a lot of time in and out of shelters before committing his life to Christ. Another person she suggested was a man who had started the soup kitchen. "He loves the shelter ministry, so we want him there for sure," Cynthia said. She went on to list others.

Martin suggested making an announcement during Sunday's holiness meeting, then approaching a few people specifically to let them know that we wanted them there. The task force affirmed this approach and made the decision to send a group email to the congregation, announce the upcoming session on Sunday morning, and ask people to send an RSVP.

The advisory council, the second group to be represented, had experienced significant growth over the past four years. Recently, they had been planning for a specific project, Youth Education Town (YET), that was starting to take shape. Funding of $1 million for the project had come in the form of a legacy gift from the National Football League. Even before the grant was awarded to The Salvation Army, a YET advisory council of more than 40 members from across North Texas had been formed. The Arlington Corps advisory council had representatives on that council. Dixon suggested that we invite the Arlington members of the YET council to the educational session. Then I suggested a particular YET member from Dallas. Mark W., vice president of an architectural firm, had mentioned to me that our YET project was interesting to him because he had designed a homeless shelter for his thesis at Iowa State. He had shared some interesting ideas with me about the way rooms could be designed to create a warmer atmosphere. Everyone at the task force agreed that he would bring a helpful perspective.

The final decision to be made was how guests from our shelter would be selected to participate. Martin gave a helpful word, "We cannot make anyone attend. If we do, it might be counterproductive. Let's allow them to choose to participate." Martin and I also expressed concern that if we left the door wide open, this could be a chance for everyone in the FLC to attend. With no contrary words from Cynthia and Dixon, Martin and I decided that we would approach certain parents and invite them.

Dixon mentioned how beneficial it had been to have former residents come to advisory council meetings and tell their stories. "Would it hurt our project if some former residents participated? They could provide a voice that speaks from the other side of homelessness." We elected to have Martin recruit at least one former resident to participate.

Why Didn't I Do This Earlier?

The task force meeting was an exciting experience for me because I could see many verbal and nonverbal connections being made among these people who represented distinct sectors of Salvation Army ministry. Most of the time, my role was to start a discussion; they kept the conversation going themselves as I furiously took notes. Though these people had had almost no interaction before this meeting, I sensed no territorialism in their conversation. On the contrary, their communication and teamwork showed that they shared the same vision.

Watching everyone work together so effectively, I couldn't help but mourn the reality that this was the first time in my four years of ministry here that these groups had ever come together. Instead, I had been working with each group as if they were separate entities. I am not sure if this separation was a selfish motivation or just the way I have been taught the Army functions. Generally, Abby and I, as corps officers, were the only link among these groups. The problems that I explain as systematically separating so-called "social" and "spiritual" ministries had made its way into my leadership and the structural way I administered the Salvation Army's mission in Arlington. The systemic structure I had inherited and perpetuated had done nothing to create a shared vision and ministry, so the corps had continued to move forward with separate tasks for distinct groups instead of with a holistic missional approach.

The task force became an opportunity for a conversation to begin that could initiate a trend away from bifurcated ministry. I observed in this meeting that the collective group brought together far more insight than I could possibly have contributed alone. Their conversation and shaping of the educational session had been liberating to them and to me.

Chapter 8

Building a Bridge Session

After we made the announcement in the holiness meeting about our upcoming Building a Bridge session, "George" approached me, his head lowered, his voice barely audible. "Cap, do you think you'd take my input at this bridge thing?" I paused for a second (though I don't think he noticed), not sure how he would contribute. He had been homeless for as long as I had known him. Because he was single and didn't have kids, he wasn't a candidate for the Family Life Center. Many people had tried to get him into housing; nothing had worked. Yet he had become increasingly involved in our congregation. He volunteered in many programs and was helpful to have as support for events at the corps. He definitely was a member of our congregation; he was active in the praxis of Salvation Army theology and becoming more alive in Christ. All this went through my head in the split second before I replied, "George, this 'bridge thing' needs to hear your voice."

Hosting the event on a Saturday before school started prevented some key staff members from attending. Then I got a response from someone I hadn't intended to invite. Through an email fluke, I had mistakenly addressed a task force email to a Cynthia O. at the area command office instead of Cynthia A. at the corps. Cynthia O. responded that she couldn't make the task force meeting but would definitely be there for the Bridge session on Aug. 20. I knew her to be helpful and resourceful, but she didn't seem to fit in any of the groups at the session. The challenge for my leadership was that I had drawn some pretty clear boxes about who should and should not attend. My mistake gave me an opportunity to think about the benefits of having people from the area command at the table. Instead of uninviting Cynthia O., I decided to invite one more area command staff member so she would not be alone. These two staff members would work with the staff from the Arlington Corps.

We had the most trouble recruiting advisory council members, primarily because of prior commitments that prevented them from attending. Dixon, highly disappointed, got involved in trying to recruit some more members, as did I. Ultimately, we did get sufficient representation from that group.

The morning of the session came. After opening in prayer, I asked each person to write answers to three questions: What is the Family Life Center? What is hospitality? What is the mission of The Salvation Army? I had allowed a certain amount of time, but it became clear that it was not enough. So we were running behind schedule from the start of the session.

Next, I gave an overview of what we would be doing for the following three hours. We had advertised the Building a Bridge session as a time for "understanding The Salvation Army, thinking about Salvation Army housing ministries, and acting on our experience." So, in my PowerPoint, I bracketed the three verbs—*understanding, thinking,* and *acting*—to emphasize what our project would be about.

Because it was the first time people from different segments of ministry in Arlington were together, I asked each person to describe his or her connection to The Salvation Army.

Dixon, our advisory council chair, spoke up first. In addition to describing his position and his family's involvement in The Salvation Army, he said he was a "lifelong person from Arlington" and that he felt "this session [and the turnout for it] is indicative of the growth of the Army over the past few years."[68]

Pat P., public relations manager for the Army's Dallas–Fort Worth Metroplex Area Command, said he had become closely connected to the life of the corps because his department had been actively involved with communicating its message. As a PR specialist, he brought a unique perspective because his primary starting point is people's perceptions of the Army.

Robert B., an advisory council member and CPA who serves on the management committee, was also an elder at a large Baptist church in town; he said he had "prayerfully considered joining" the advisory council.

Millie H., another advisory council member, said she had come on board when she retired and wanted to find an organization in which to invest time.

"Beth" was the first shelter guest to speak, and I was interested to hear if she would disclose her residential status. I thought it was critical that she allow this to be known, but I was uncertain if she and other residents would feel intimidated. I need not have worried. She opened by saying, "I'm Betty and I'm with the Family Life Center; I'm a resident, and I'm totally grateful for the program."

Task force member Cynthia A. introduced herself as a sixth-generation Salvationist who was "born into The Salvation Army and loves its mission and ministry." She said the reason she loves the Army is that it is "God with hands."

Jared G. represented two groups: he was both a soldier and a part-time employee who worked with the after-school program. He said that his family has been involved with The Salvation Army for "at least four generations."

"Dean" was the first adherent to speak. Again, I was curious to see how he would describe himself; I knew that drugs, alcohol, and homelessness had filled many years of his life. He didn't mention those things or his experience working at the Union Gospel Mission. Instead, he described himself as "a member here—an adherent—who helps out wherever I can."

Kasey C., a staff member who oversees youth service programs, in effect serving as a youth pastor, said she had attended a non-denominational mega-church in Arlington before becoming active in The Salvation Army's congregation.

Mark W., the architect who served on the YET advisory council, said his firm "is known for building a little football stadium [the AT&T stadium, where the Dallas Cowboys play] down the street." Then he said that his architectural career had begun when he designed a shelter for the homeless. "That is probably where my heart is, rather than [with] a three million-square-foot football stadium. That's why I'm here," he said. I was surprised to see that Mark had brought his fiancé with him. He introduced her by saying, "She has as big of [a] heart as I do."

Pat B. described himself as a volunteer for The Salvation Army and a member of the congregation by virtue of playing in the band. This was a key moment of ontological identity because Pat was a person who tithed, participated, and volunteered, but was not technically a member of the corps.

Pat's wife, Peggy, was another surprise addition to the session. She said she was not a member of the congregation. "It's not that I dislike or don't want to be part of [The] Salvation Army; it's just not where my home is," she said. "I was born and bred a Methodist; I'm probably going to die a Methodist." With an extensive background in human services, however, Peggy was able to contribute in the session.

Richard, also known as "Moses," was an active adherent. He had become a Christian while in prison. His hairstyle, beard, tattoos, and rough voice sometimes caused him to be stereotyped as a troublemaker. For much of his life, he had been, but now he was as caring and compassionate as anyone in the corps. He said, "I'm involved in the soup line ... and do whatever I can around here."

Bill T. was one of two soldiers who had been a part of the corps when Abby and I arrived. A fourth-generation Salvationist, Bill said that his "grandmother used to wash the shirts of the Founder [William Booth]."

George, the homeless man mentioned at the beginning of this chapter, described himself as a "member and adherent. I also volunteer every Saturday night at the soup kitchen ... I call this place my home." George chose not to mention his own homelessness.

"Alberto," a new soldier, said he had become active through the Adult Rehabilitation Center in Fort Worth. He owned his own painting business and volunteered a lot of time at the corps.

I was surprised when "Bobby" walked in. He and his wife were living in the shelter, and his wife had left him just five days before the session. He described himself as "the only resident in the room who is a single parent [of a teenage daughter] ... and a single male parent at that."

"Lashonda," the only former resident of the FLC, said with pride, "I used to be a resident ... I'm here today because I don't know what I would have done without The Salvation Army ... this is the least I could do."

Bill M., a case coordinator for the FLC, was a retired mortgage banker who described himself as a "former" sixth-generation Salvationist. He said, "Over a period of several years, the Lord has led me back to The Salvation Army." Although he and his wife were active at a large Baptist church, Bill also attended the Salvation Army's (or Corps') worship services on a biweekly basis.

Task force member Martin J. talked about his experience with the homeless community and his role at the FLC and the corps.

"Sandra" identified herself as an FLC resident. She was the mother of nine children, eight of whom had been living with her in a car before she came with them to the shelter.

Kristin V., vice chair of the YET advisory council, was as close to royalty in Arlington as anyone could be. She was the daughter-in-law of a man who had been mayor for more than 20 years and owned several car dealerships. Kristin and her husband were actively involved in the community.

Captain Abby Miller talked about the distinct role she plays as an officer appointed to the Army's work in Arlington. She said she was thankful that the Army had allowed flexibility in her schedule to care for our three children under the age of 4.

The extended period of introductions allowed the group to find common ground and gravitate toward the shared purpose of the project.

Giving some time to allow people to share their first impressions of the Army was also helpful. I had in mind a vision of Salvation Army mission that I hoped would unite the group, but I wanted that perspective to flow from the participants' experience and understanding.

Before I finished the question, "What was your first impression of The Salvation Army?" Pat B.'s hand shot up. "Social services. I had no idea it was an actual church … " Several people were nodding in agreement. Others started gesturing with their hands as if they were ringing bells and mentioned red kettles and thrift stores as points of contact with the Army.

Cynthia then took the floor and said, in a didactic way, "People always see us in that one little aspect [family stores] … we want to communicate that we are a church—first and foremost, we are primarily an evangelical part of the Christian church." The "first and foremost" language is used often in Salvation Army congregations throughout the world, but when Cynthia said that, it struck me in a different way because I was thinking about the staff, advisory council members, and guests of the shelter, for whom the Army is not their church home. I sensed that this statement could be taken by other groups as marginalizing their affiliation with the Army.

Normally, such phrases have simply floated by my consciousness, but the reality of bringing these diverse groups together had forced me to re-examine the way I understood how The Salvation Army functions as a church. If by "first and foremost," we mean that we are a congregation with Sunday school classes and offering plates, then we miss the depth of Salvation Army ecclesiology. If, however, "first and foremost" means that every aspect of Army activity is a part of God's mission to save and redeem the world, then yes, we are first and foremost a people of God and hence a church.

I took some time to emphasize the international mission statement, which gave me the opportunity to talk about the localization and adaptability of the Army's work in at least 123 countries. I also affirmed that "preaching the Gospel of Jesus Christ" is not done only by clergy/officers but by all who consider themselves a part of The Salvation Army.

I was the primary presenter for the session, but I asked Martin to talk about the essential functions of the Family Life Center. In his limited time, he communicated the program requirements and talked about our partner agencies and the basic way the FLC strategizes to move families toward stability. He was exceptionally clear, at my request, in differentiating between transitional shelters like the FLC and emergency shelters.

I then showed a video about a single dad and his son who had come through the shelter program and were now in their own home.

Next, it was time to venture into my presentation on hospitality as a paradigm for Salvation Army mission. I opened with a question, "When you hear the word *hospitality,* what does that make you think of?" The first answer came quickly from Kasey: "Hotels." Bill added, "Being welcomed." Others commented about having people over to their homes, making food, and creating a welcoming environment. Moses added that it was "receiving people with a smile." Dixon brought up a connection to hospitals.

Then came a moment for which I did not plan. Bill raised his hand to say, "George wants to know what the word *metaphor* means." The slide on the screen during the discussion had the title, "Hospitality as a Metaphor for Salvation Army Mission."

George asked, "Yeah, Cap, what is a metaphor?"

The words stumbled out of my mouth. "Oh ... that's the way we describe something we don't understand ... so ... you can use something else to describe another reality. Like ..."

Others in the room felt that I was searching for a good explanation. Kasey, trained as an elementary school teacher, piped in, "It's like an eagle is a symbol of freedom."

I agreed with her, but I still felt the explanation was lacking. I began questioning the validity of my use of the word metaphor. Was hospitality really a metaphor for social services? Was that what I was going for in this session? I contemplated changing the word to *paradigm,* but I realized that word could confuse people even more. Though my mind was still spinning, I said, "Hospitality is a way we can look at the reality of Salvation Army housing ministries."

Then I said, "George, I'm so glad you asked that question. So if I say a word that you don't get, let me know." With a satisfied nod, George said,

"Thanks, Cap."

This was a key moment in my project because it brought to light for me personally that hospitality is not merely a metaphor but a Christian practice.

I moved forward, much more conscious of the words I had used in my PowerPoint and offering explanations of terms along the way. After discussing the root of the word *hospitality* to mean essentially "love of strangers," we moved to the discussion of hospitality in Scripture. I showed some passages on a slide and asked groups to study them. But the font was too small, so I had to read out the passage reference to each group. More confusion came because some people didn't have Bibles. I thought this segment was taking too long, but on review of the videotape, I saw that it had lasted only seven minutes. Each group shared what they had learned and made strong reflections on the passages.

In my summary of the New Testament passages and concepts of hospitality, I underscored how they named explicitly what had been implicit in the Old Testament passages. I used this language because the move from implicit to explicit was a motif I wanted to employ as a template for Salvation Army theological praxis. I then connected the tradition of hospitality in the New Testament with Christian tradition by saying, "What is interesting is that this understanding that comes from Scripture, this word from Scripture, was passed on to the early church. One of the reasons that happened was the intersection of house and church."

Sandra, a shelter guest, raised her hand.

"I am sorry to interrupt, but this Salvation Army program ... it's the only place that has accommodations for a family of my size. I am a single mother with eight children. When we went to other shelters, they wanted me to separate my family. They wanted me to leave my 11-year-old son, who has special needs, in the men's dorm by hisself [sic]. And

I couldn't do it. But The Salvation Army welcomed us and they have a facility that can accommodate a family this large. It's wonderful. I am sorry for interrupting."

I said, "Oh … interrupt me like that anytime."

Sandra reiterated that there was no shelter in the metroplex that could accommodate a family of her size. When she said this, I realized that I had left out the fact that our program is distinct in the area as a family shelter.

Bobby said that as a single father with a teenage daughter, there was no other shelter that would take him.

Though the comments didn't come at the best time, I thought that the testimonies came to the surface then because the shelter residents heard the way their stories fit into the biblical mandate to show hospitality.

I then went into Army history, noting that in the beginning, there was no dual focus on social and spiritual ministry. I highlighted several important dates and summarized the evolution of Army activity through the institution of the social wing and the publication of *In Darkest England.* (See Chapter 3.) Gently exposing the bifurcation of Salvation Army ministry was a delicate subject. I suggested:

One of the problems that can happen in Salvation Army ministry is that we can move away from understanding why we do what we do. All of us. Me. Because we are a social service entity, we provide services to people, as opposed to understanding the reality that we serve real people who are just like us. Instead, we want to restore the relational dimensions to social services, and that is what I need your help with in the next hour.

I concluded this segment by talking about the benefits that hospitality can offer as a way to look at the housing ministry of the Arlington Corps. I touched on the themes of hospitality: acknowledging the dignity of others; recognizing Jesus in every stranger; and moving beyond a service provided to the person served. Finally, I used a famous quote from William Booth that had the potential of uniting the people in the room behind a purpose:

> While women weep, as they do now, I'll fight; while little children go hungry, as they do now, I'll fight; while men go to prison, in and out, in and out, as they do now, I'll fight; while there is a drunkard left, while there is a poor girl on the streets, while there remains one lost soul without the light of God, I'll fight—I'll fight to the very end!

Conversations in the FLC

Then it was time for the tour of the Family Life Center. As we approached the stairs, I encouraged each participant to visualize coming up to the doors at the lowest time in their lives. This imaginative leap helped people to find solidarity with the families served at the FLC.

Several unexpected benefits came from the tour. I had wondered how it could work for approximately 30 people. I found myself taking advantage of open spaces to speak to the group as a whole. There were wonderfully helpful conversations happening among the groups. What intuitively occurred was that guests of our shelter dispersed equally around the group. It was almost as if each guest or former guest was acting as a mini tour guide.

I was surprised to learn that not every member of the corps congregation had received a formal tour of the FLC. Many were aware of the ministry and could point out where the shelter was, but I heard comments like, "I always wondered what the rooms looked like," and "I didn't know that we had a pantry."

The tour also gave me the opportunity to provide specific details about how the shelter operates. As we walked through the computer room, for example, the shelter guests and I talked about the importance of job training and learning to use the Internet for job searches. Seeing the security monitor station gave me an opportunity to illustrate the importance of our security system. When we toured the kitchen, we saw the pragmatic reality of feeding a family when 15 other families are present.

Participants knew that it would soon be their turn to speak, but they were uncertain about the role they would play. It was time to move to the brainstorming session.

Chapter 9

Brainstorming
and Meeting with Teens

Now it was time for the brainstorming session, but I first needed to clarify our objective. I said, "Mark, as an architect, might think that taking down a wall or adding a sunroof might improve the shelter environment, but we are looking for ideas that can be done and measured in two weeks."

Cynthia said, "I need some clarity about what type of idea you are looking for."

I said that we were looking for ideas in four different categories: the facility, the way we name our services, programs (such as food service, case management, classes), and how the groups represented at the meeting could interact with other groups that make up the Arlington Corps.

Once the participants separated into the subgroups with which they were primarily associated, I asked them to appoint a recorder and assured everyone that "there are no bad ideas."

One of the most rewarding aspects of this time for me was walking around the room while the groups buzzed with conversation; it was affirming to hear that they grasped the concepts I had presented, and I saw that they were being very creative.

Because of the short amount of time left in the session, I asked the groups to present the two ideas they agreed to be most significant. Kasey was the first to present for the staff. Saying that the steps leading up to the FLC are "high, intimidating, ugly, and possibly scary to small children," she suggested that an encouraging Scripture be painted on the staircase. The group's second idea concerned the room numbers for shelter guests. Kasey said, "Is there a good reason it says 'FLC–101' and 'FLC–102'? I mean, we know it is the FLC, and do we really need three digits?

I responded that the a possible reason for the numbers was that the building was originally to have been two levels high, but there was "no particular reason that we have three numbers."

Kasey went on to say that the staff also refer to the residents by room numbers. Her group wanted the rooms to be renamed with inspirational names or for influential people, "like the William Booth room or the Grace room."

Cynthia, representing the congregation, said her group had also selected the concept of renaming rooms. They said the rooms could be called something like the "agape" room, or they could be named after the books of the Bible. The group's second idea concerned corps members' interaction with shelter guests. The suggestion was that there could be an "adopt–a–family" program, where members of the congregation adopt families in the shelter. David expanded on the concept: "We could have people over to our house for a weekend so they don't have to be in the shelter all weekend."

The shelter guests were up next. Their first concept was to host a "parents' night in," which would be a time when volunteers could watch the guests' children so the parents could play games or watch a movie together. The second proposal involved some problems with the use of the communal refrigerator, but in the end, Martin and I suggested that this concern should be addressed but would be better taken up in a residents' meeting at the shelter.

The advisory organizations group presented last. Their first idea was to create a more welcoming entrance that would reduce "the barrier of the stairs." Their second idea was to "soften the environment with plants and other means that blur the necessary security lines between the different zones of the housing area."

I saw that two ideas had been mentioned more than once. The first idea I proposed, in order to form a consensus, was the staff's recommendation to paint a Scripture verse on the stairs. I opened the floor for discussion. Sandra said, "I think it needs more than a Scripture verse; I think the whole thing needs to be painted." I asked Alberto, who is a painter, if this task could be completed in two weeks. He affirmed that this was possible, and the group then agreed that this was the first idea we would implement.

The second idea I proposed was to do something different with the naming of the rooms. Both the congregation and the staff had made this recommendation, and the advisory council had made a suggestion about improving the atmosphere inside the building.

A flurry of conversation began, and it went on for quite a while. Because the noon hour was upon us, I asked the group to stay for an additional 15 minutes, and they all agreed. Noting that we had been working with a few concepts, I asked whether we should use biblical names, historical names, or concepts like grace or agape.

Mark took a prominent role in the discussion. He felt we should have individual names on the doors of people's rooms.

When I was doing research for my thesis, I found that homeless shelters have a big gap in how they connect with people. There are barriers that people have to go through as they enter a building, which, by its nature, needs to be secure. What I found is that adding a personal touch that gives someone ownership helps with this problem.

Kasey added, "One of our group's other ideas was to add a sign that says 'home away from home.' That might create a more hospitable environment." A number of people were nodding their heads in agreement, but another contingent obviously disagreed.

Lashonda was the first to speak up about putting names on the door. She confidently jolted the rest of the group, including me, who had thought we were onto something.

> The problem with that is that this [The Salvation Army] is not my home. Though I love and appreciate all that The Salvation Army has done for me, it is just a transition. The FLC is getting me from one place to another. While I was here, there were some people who were treating this like their home, and they were not the ones working hard to find a job and get out of here. I think it [the shelter] should be an encouraging place, but it shouldn't be too nice.

Other guests agreed with Lashonda. Sandra said, "I definitely don't think of this place as a home away from home. It is more of a home on the way to a home."

Mark was obviously shocked. He asked the guests, "Don't you think you would feel better about your situation if you had your name on the door or something you could make your own?"

Bluntly, Sandra, Lashonda, and Bobby responded in unison: "No!" Bobby added, "Not really. I see what you are saying, but I agree with LaShonda."

To complicate the situation, Beth, another guest, commented that she thought adding something personal "could be nice." The conversation went on for another few minutes, with the group as a whole seeming to be surprised by the guests' response. Their input was precisely the reason the task force had sought to include shelter guests in addition to other groups representing the Arlington Corps.

The discussion was intense enough that I concluded its trajectory would take us beyond the time allotted. I decided to appoint a committee to investigate details of naming the rooms. I asked for volunteers; most who raised their hands were shelter guests, with a few from the corps congregation volunteering to participate.

The last order of business, after I thanked everyone for their participation, was to have participants complete a short assessment of the day. I asked them to write new answers to our original questions: "What is the Family Life Center?" "What is hospitality?" "What is the mission of The Salvation Army?"

As people handed in their answers, I had another opportunity to thank participants individually. I was frustrated to hear a response from three members of the corps congregation, who said, "We had all the exact same answers [as we had in] the beginning." I didn't take the remark to mean, "Thanks for nothing; we didn't learn anything," but rather that they felt they had already understood all the concepts presented. The remark was in the same spirit of Cynthia's "The Salvation Army is first and foremost a church." I recognized the tone because I resonate with it myself, but I was discouraged that these congregation members were not able to identify any growth in understanding. One participant even showed me his page, where he had written in large letters, "NO CHANGE."

I reflected that I hadn't spent much time in creating an assessment tool for the session, and that could have been the root of the problem. But overall, I felt that the session had been a positive experience that would lead to immediate renewal in the Arlington Corps' theological praxis. It also had positioned every group active in the life of the corps to act from a missional foundation in the future.

Teen Session

This session was set up to be an hour–long discussion with the six youth aged 13 and over living in the FLC. My approach was to use the same PowerPoint with the teens as a guide, but I altered my presentation style by using stories and engaging the teens' experiences and impressions.

I started with the question, "What was your first impression of The Salvation Army?" Immediately, "Kevin," a 14–year–old from a large family, muttered under his breath, "A dump."[69] The others made noises as if he had just done something terrible. "Karen" elbowed her brother, "You can't say that in front of the captain."

I told the kids that I was very interested in their thoughts, whether positive or negative. "This is a time that I get to hear what you really think. I am not saying I am going to be able to make everything better here, but I think we can do some things [to help]." I then asked Kevin, "Can you tell me what you mean by 'a dump'"?

He shrugged his shoulders but eventually responded,

> Well, I mean, well, I wasn't talking about *this* Salvation Army. You asked, 'What did you first think of The Salvation Army?' and I did not even know that [it] existed until we went to the Salvation Army [in another city]. That place was scary; it *was* a dump. It was like they didn't want any kids there or something. We had to sleep on the floor. I like this place; I've got my own bed here and we have a TV.

Three youth in the room had also been referred to our program through that shelter, and they each nodded their heads, affirming the distinction Kevin had made.

I asked next what the teens' first impressions of our shelter had been.

"It was kind of scary; the lights were out when I came," "Du" said. "The hallway is long, and I was worried for me and my mom." Du and his mom were from Vietnam; before coming to our shelter, she had been in an abusive relationship classified as human trafficking. It was from this situation that she and her son found refuge at the FLC.

A few other kids responded as the adults had, talking about thrift stores and bell-ringers. The final response came from 16-year-old "Jacob," who said "The Salvation Army is a place where you can get back on your feet."

As I came to a slide in the presentation about William Booth, they were quick to make fun. "Who is that old guy with a beard?" Kevin said "Yeah, they had a gold thing of that old guy at the Salvation Army [in the other city], and it said something about fighting. I used to like to read it." Interestingly enough, the slide about Booth's "I'll fight" speech was up next. I read it aloud. Kyle said, "Yeah, that's it!" I asked the group how those words made them feel.

"David," a 13-year-old African-American boy who was in the shelter with his mother, answered, "It makes me feel so good because it makes me feel like they [The Salvation Army] will not give up on us, like they will stand up for us." This was an encouraging turn for the group and the dynamics of the youth session.

There was no need for a tour of the shelter, where the teens lived, so we moved to the brainstorming session. The teens had several ideas that ranged from repairing vacuum cleaners to getting more DVDs. Then David spoke up. "I always worry about that cement on the front hill; what's it called? Oh, yeah, the foundation. I worry if all that dirt goes away, the shelter could have damage." This was an interesting observation because the source of his concern could have just been something out of the ordinary that Daniel had observed, or it could have reflected his not feeling settled in this place and a metaphorical picture of what he was longing for in a home.

The group tended toward ideas that would enable them to leave their own mark on the shelter. One suggestion was to paint the walls and make a place for them to sign their names. This idea morphed into painting ceiling tiles in the lounge area. These tiles could have their names on them, and every teen who came through the shelter would have an opportunity to add a ceiling tile. "Samantha" responded to the idea in a way that summarized the session well: "If we do that, there could someday be lots of tiles, and new kids would know that others have gone through tough times too. Maybe we could come back and talk to those kids after we get in our houses."

So a third idea, this one from the teens, was added to the plan for making our housing ministry fulfill the vision of true Christian hospitality.

Chapter 10
Best–Laid Plans

We started out with the mandate to implement three changes in the Family Life Center within two weeks. That didn't happen.

The committee to name the rooms and the lounge area couldn't find a time when all the initial volunteers could meet. After two months of trying, I elected to set a date for Martin and me to meet with the residents who had attended the Building a Bridge session. The Bridge session had taken place on Aug. 20; the committee finally met on Nov. 15. After a good discussion, we decided to use names that had a spiritual connection but not necessarily names from the Bible. We named the rooms Abraham, Bethel, Barnabas, Bethany, Caleb, Esther, Faith, Grace, Isaiah, Joshua, Jordan, Mary, Martha, and Ruth.

The best discussion came as we deliberated over the name of the lounge area. For many years, it had been called Bright Space, after a foundation, Bright Spaces, that had at one time provided toys for the room. We tried to contact the foundation but were unable to. I felt confident that we could give the room a new name. The committee decided on the Living Room. Betty commented, " … everybody, no matter what religion you are, has a living room. It is more homey … that's what we call it when I go to the house and get all the family together. I mean, we go to the house; we sit down; we play cards, and we watch movies. It's all done in that one room."

After the meeting, the new names were attached to the doors and new artwork was placed at the entrance of the Living Room. An email went out to corps staff detailing the changes and emphasizing that guests should no longer be referred to by room number.

The second project, painting the stairs leading to the FLC and adding a Scripture verse, was also delayed. We found that the staircase was difficult to paint because it required a very specific type of cement paint. The lowest bid to do the job came in at $1,700; because our budget was tight at the end of the fiscal year, I decided to wait until after Oct. 1 to move forward. The stairs were completed Oct. 4.

The next phase of the project was to paint a Scripture verse on each of the 11 stairs. We invited an artist who had done murals for a large Baptist church to help us. She was willing, and she even laid out a computerized design. But she was unable to follow through because of scheduling problems. In early November she sent word that she wouldn't be able to complete the project before the end of the year.

So we went in another direction. The entire senior class—about 50 students—from a private high school in town came to our corps yearly in early November for a day of service learning. I called the art teacher at the school to ask her to select a group of students who could help us with the stairs. The students enthusiastically completed the project in one day, but the next day, a downpour washed all their work away. It was a blessing that a half–dozen students volunteered to come back after school later that week and recreate their artwork.

The third project was completed at the end of October. Kasey Carrell, who had become our student minister, led an evening when the teens painted their own tiles in the Living Room.

While our "best–laid" plan to complete all the changes within two weeks of the Bridge session had not come to fruition, I was thankful that our staff persisted to complete the projects, which gave me the opportunity to assess whether these ideas could refresh the theological praxis of the Salvation Army's housing ministry in Arlington.

Did the changes make a difference?

An initial survey of the guests and FLC staff was done in the beginning of October. A final survey of the same groups was given out on Dec. 12, and all the surveys came back before the end of the year.

One question asked of the guests in the survey was whether they felt that the "rooms, facility, and food create a welcoming atmosphere." Before our changes were implemented, the average score, on a scale of 10, with 10 being the highest mark, was 7.66. After implementation, the average jumped to 9.28. Nothing had changed at the shelter except the renaming of the rooms and living room and the painting of the stairs and the ceiling tiles. This change in score indicated to me that these small alterations had made a difference in guests' perception of the Family Life Shelter as a welcoming place.

Another survey question was, "Which description best explains your understanding of the Family Life Center: an emergency housing program, an outreach of the Salvation Army's church, a government program, a transitional shelter?" Before implementation of the changes, most saw the FLC as a transitional shelter. After implementation, an equal number of people circled transitional shelter and outreach of the Salvation Army church. It is reasonable to conclude that biblical names on the rooms and the Scripture on the stairs helped guests to connect the ecclesiological dimensions of the shelter to its functional aspects.

A question asked of the staff was, "Have you ever referred to guests by room number?" with a follow-up question, "Were you instructed to do this or is it something that makes communication easier?" Four of the six staff members who answered the questions said they had referred to guests by room number, largely because of confidentiality issues. After implementation of the room name changes, four staff members said they would still use room numbers to identify guests, and two said they had not done so since the room names were added. Interestingly, the guests' perceptions were quite different from the staff's. In the first survey, guests were asked if they had been identified by room number and how that had made them feel. More than half said they had been, and comments ranged from feeling OK about it to making them feel like cellmates. But after the rooms received names, 100 percent of the guests perceived that they had not been referred to by room numbers, even though some staff said they had still used numbers as identification. That spoke to me of a change in staff attitude.

That attitude shift was reflected in another question asked of guests: "How does the staff do at treating your family with dignity and respect?" Before the changes were implemented, nine guests who answered the question gave an average score of 7.66. Those who gave lower scores (under five) made comments like, "Some of them need to work on people skills." "Some workers at [the] front desk and kitchen ... make you feel like less than a person." "Some staff ... talk about you and laugh like you are a second-class citizen." Those who gave higher scores on the question said that they found the staff welcoming; that they never felt treated as if they were homeless. After the changes were made in the FLC, six respondents gave an average score on the question of 9.83. Guests made comments like "[They] always showed respect and kindness toward us." "We are not looked down upon." "The staff make it known that they truly care."

The survey posed another question that turned out to be directly related to our project: "On a scale of 1 to 10, how welcoming is the entrance to the Family Life Center?" The average answer on the pre-survey was 6.66. Guests commented, "There is a lot more that could be done to make it more welcoming." "Just looks like a building. Nothing that really pops out at you till you get in the building and meet all the people." "Some say [it] is unwelcoming." In the post-survey, after the stairs had been painted, the average score of the six people who answered was 9.16. Comments shed light on the improved score. "It is better than before." "Very [welcoming]! Especially now with the Scripture on the steps."

That verse, "Come to me, all you who are weary and burdened, and I will give you rest" (Matthew 11:28) offered a promise of true holistic Christian hospitality. This renewal was emerging because all the stakeholders connected to the Arlington Salvation Army had been given space to live out Jesus' mandate.

Chapter 11
Reflections

This project encouraged me to discover biblical, theological, and theoretical reasons why The Salvation Army has entered a ministry like the Family Life Center and how the paradigm of hospitality might fuel renewal and consistency in the way we approached this ministry. What I discovered was that focusing and clarifying missional hospitality—the foundation for such ministries—could encourage and electrify all the groups that make up the Army and bring a renewed theological praxis to Arlington's housing ministry.

The session, "Building a Bridge: Thinking, Acting, and Understanding God's Mission for the Salvation Army's Family Life Center," provided an environment in which participants from all facets of the life of the Arlington Corps—staff, congregation members, advisory organizations members, and guests of the shelter—could hear about a new approach to ministry all at once. Those participating in the session played in the symphony of Salvation Army ministry; rather than rehearsing their separate parts backstage, they performed together. The uniting of missional participants was one of the clear victories of this project.

When explicitly biblical ideas emerged in the implementation phase— the naming of rooms and writing a Scripture verse on the stairs of the shelter—the shelter guests said that they felt more welcomed, dignified, and respected. The guests also began to recognize this ministry as connected to the ecclesiological identify of The Salvation

Army. The ministry was renewed as a beautiful expression of Christian hospitality.

It was stunning to me that my homeless friend George very simply and powerfully changed my thinking about the way to apply hospitality to the Salvation Army's ministry. When he asked what a metaphor was, I realized the truth that hospitality is not a metaphor at all. It is a practice that is thoroughly a part of Christian history. The Building a Bridge session was meant to inspire people to actually participate in loving strangers and to practice hospitality with them.

I am thankful for the opportunity to "do something" about my theological convictions regarding Salvation Army ministry and the Christian practice of hospitality.

Commissioner George Scott Railton, an early Army pioneer, challenged the fledgling movement in the words of this hymn:

> Through the world resounding,
> Let the gospel sounding,
> Summon all, at Jesus' call,
> His glorious cross surrounding.
> Sons of God, earth's trifles leaving,
> Be not faithless but believing;
> To your conquering captain cleaving,
> Forward to the Fight.[70]

Salvation Army hospitality is missional. It is connected to God's plan to redeem the world. It calls the soldiers and officers of The Salvation Army to compassionately move "Forward to the Fight." I encourage you to join the battle.

Epilogue

I could feel it in my toes and in my heart. During the first few seconds of standing in front of people I was appointed to lead at the "Building a Bridge" event in Arlington. I knew that I would never look at Salvation Army ministry the same. In those seconds I realized that my advisory board hat, shelter administrator hat, pastor hat, and supervisor hat should not be interchanged and that I should not be the only connecting link among these groups. In that moment I realized that a part of my calling is to bring together various sectors of The Salvation Army to create a unified vision.

Currently a task force is working toward a "Building a Bridge" event for The Salvation Army of Gwinnett County, Georgia, where I am currently serving. This task force is developing a session that will engage our congregation, staff, advisors, graduates, and households in our Home Sweet Home program. Instead of being called "Building a Bridge," the name for the education event in Arlington, the Gwinnett task force chose the name "Be the Bridge." Already the task force is taking the model project we implemented in Arlington in directions I could have not anticipated.

One practical outgrowth of this project is to think about hospitality as a concept that can be applied far beyond housing ministries. Every aspect of Christian witness can be seen as offering hospitality. Our community centers, Boys and Girls Clubs, senior programs, character-building activities, music ensembles, after-school programs, music conservatories, camping programs, hospitals, food pantries, emergency assistance offices, schools, angel tree programs, red kettle fundraising, major gift management, planned giving operations, legal services, and even headquarters administration can be renewed through the lens of holistic hospitality.

I believe too that a practical event, such as "Building a Bridge," could be used to refocus and unite each of these ministries for the fight.

It is my prayer that this study and project will enable the Gospel of Jesus Christ to be welcomed into more lives as we offer a holistic hospitality to the world.

Endnotes

1. Christine D. Pohl, *Making Room: Recovering Hospitality as a Christian Tradition* (Grand Rapids: Eerdmans, 1999), p. 20.

2. Pohl, p. 20.

3. Laurence W. Wood, *The Meaning of Pentecost in Early Methodism: Rediscovering John Fletcher as John Wesley's Vindicator and Designated Successor* (Lanham, MA: The Scarecrow Press, 2002), pp.145–162.

4. Pohl, p. 162.

5. I use the word *holistic* to identify an effective balance in mission between personal and corporate, spiritual and physical aspects of ministry.

6. William Booth, *East London Evangelist,* October 1868, p. 3. Quoted in Pamela J. Walker, *Pulling the Devil's Kingdom Down: The Salvation Army in Victorian Britain* (Berkley, CA: University of California Press, 2001), pp. 41–42.

7. William Booth, *In Darkest England and the Way Out* (Atlanta: The Salvation Army, 1984), p. 24. This term referred to the tenth of society that was suffering from the negative consequences of the Industrial Revolution.

8. An overview of the Victorian environment in which The Salvation Army operated is discussed in R. David Rightmire's book, *Sacraments and*

The Salvation Army: Pneumatological Foundations (Metuchen, NJ: The Scarecrow Press, 1990), p. 31ff.

9. Philip D. Needham, *Redemption and Social Reformation: A Theological Study of William Booth and His Movement.* Unpublished M.Th. thesis (Princeton Theological Seminary, 1967), p. 2.

10. William Booth, in George Scott Railton, *Twenty-One Years Salvation Army* (London: The Salvation Army, 1886), p. 22.

11. Robert Sandall, *The History of The Salvation Army* (London: The Salvation Army 1947–2000. Vols. 1–3 by Sandall; vols. 4–5 by Arch Wiggins; vol. 6 by Frederick Coutts; vol. 7 by Henry Gariepy), vol. 2, p. 338.

12. Roger J. Green, *War on Two Fronts: The Redemptive Theology of William Booth* (Atlanta: The Salvation Army, 1989), pp. 40–75.

13. Some scholars, notably K.S. Inglis and Norman H. Murdoch, have proposed that William Booth's move to include social ministries was purely motivated by his failure of not having reached the poorest of the poor with the Gospel, particularly in the East End, in the 1880s. I sharply disagree with this historical interpretation. Recently R.G. Moyles has made a similar claim that is unsubstantiated in *Come Join Our Army: Historical Reflections on Salvation Army Growth* (Alexandria: Crest Books, 2007), 127-134. For a detailed response to Murdoch and Inglis see my *Missional Hospitality: Toward a Renewed Theological Praxis in Salvation Army Housing Ministries,* unpublished D.Min. dissertation (Southern Methodist University, 2012), pp 13-17, and Roger J. Green, "Theological Roots of In Darkest England and the Way Out," *Wesleyan Theological Journal* (1990, 25:1).

14. Sandall, vol. 2, p. 338.

15. Ann. M. Woodall, *What Price the Poor? William Booth, Karl Marx and the*

London Residuum (Burlington, VT: Ashgate, 2005), pp. 150–153.

16. Sandall, vol. 3, pp. 3–10. See also Roger J. Green, "A Historical Salvation Army Perspective," in *Creed and Deed: Toward a Christian Theology of Social Services in The Salvation Army,* ed. John D. Waldron (Oakville, Ontario: The Salvation Army Triumph Press, 1995), p. 51.

17. This exposure happened through a deliberate plan that resulted in the imprisonment of Stead. Jenty Fairbank gives a detailed account of this event in "Saving a Girl for Seven Pounds," the second chapter of *Booth's Boots: Social Service Beginnings in The Salvation Army* (London: The Salvation Army, 1983). Frederick Coutts also details the event in "Truth Fallen in the Street," the fourth chapter of *Bread for My Neighbor: The Social Influence of William Booth* (London: Hodder and Stoughton, 1978), pp. 45–62. Donald W. Dayton also writes about this event in his important book about the social activisim of the holiness movement: *Discovering an Evangelical Heritage* (Hendrickson Publishers, 1976), p. 17.

18. Fairbank, p. 131.

19. Pamela J. Walker, *Pulling the Devil's Kingdom Down: The Salvation Army in Victorian England* (Berkeley, CA: University of California Press, 2001), p. 239.

20. William Booth, "Salvation for Both Worlds," *All the World* (January 1989), p. 6.

21. Booth, "Salvation for Both Worlds," p. 2.

22. Sandall, vol. 3, pp. 101–104.

23. William Booth, *In Darkest England and the Way Out.* The "scheme" consisted of three proposals. First, the City Colony (pp. 102–135), where ragged, poor, hungry men and women from the city could be housed,

trained, and helped upwards to honorable and useful lives. The second proposal was the Farm Colony (pp. 136–153), a place where those who sought assistance in agricultural work could be provided with appropriate training. The final proposal was the Over–Seas Colony (pp. 154–165), which was to be a self–supported group working from various countries to assist each other. Other ideas were offered toward social relief (pp. 166–245). Booth concluded by showing how the structure of The Salvation Army was well–suited to accomplish this social scheme (pp. 249–287).

24. Booth implicitly advocated an economic view of the Trinity that sees each person of the Trinity as distinct in their roles and interpersonal relationships while sharing in one divine nature. Hence, each person of the Trinity is involved in stages of salvation. The holiness movement of the 19th century began to emphasize the role of the Holy Spirit in the process of salvation and sanctification. The source of this emphasis (in both the holiness movement and Booth's thinking) is undoubtedly John Fletcher and the later writing of John Wesley. See Wood, pp. 126–134, 313–336.

25. This theme is more thoroughly developed in Andrew S. Miller III, *The Good Time Coming: The Impact of William Booth's Eschatological Vision*, unpublished M.Div. thesis (Asbury Theological Seminary, 2005), pp. 21–26.

26. William Booth, "The Millenium [sic] or, The Ultimate Triumph of Salvation Army Principles," *All the World* (August 1890), p. 343.

27. For more on this, see Andrew S. Miller III, "Escatological Ethics: The Army's Hospitable Legacy," *Word and Deed* (November 2007), Vol. 10:1, pp. 39–60.

28. Booth, "Salvation for Both Worlds," pp. 2–3. This quote is parallel to the imagery of Fletcher and Wesley, who often used "promised land" analogies. It also demonstrates that within Booth's theology, there is no dichotomy between the work of the Son and the work of the Spirit.

29. Edward H. McKinley, *Marching to Glory: The History of The Salvation Army in the United States* (Grand Rapids: Eerdmans, 1986), pp. 41–43.

30. *The War Cry* (October 1886).

31. *The War Cry* (October 1886)

32. Edward H. McKinley, *Somebody's Brother: A History of the Salvation Army's Men's Social Service Department, 1891–1985* (Lewiston, NY: Edwin Mellen Press Limited, 1986), pp. 41–43.

33. McKinley, *Somebody's Brother,* p. 54.

34. McKinley, *Marching to Glory,* p. 177, and Beatrice Combs, "Social Services: Women," ed. John G. Merritt, *The Historical Dictionary of The Salvation Army* (Lanham, MA: The Scarecrow Press), p. 533.

35. Quoted in McKinley, *Marching to Glory,* p. 178.

36. Combs, in *The Historical Dictionary of The Salvation Army,* p. 637.

37. *The Salvation Army Year Book 2012* (London: The Salvation Army International Headquarters, 2012), 29-31.

38. Frank Smith, in *The War Cry,* Dec. 25, 1886. Quoted in McKinley, *Somebody's Brother,* p. 6.

39. Fred Cox, "The Founder," special lecture to cadets on Jan. 4, 1924, p. 9, quoted in Green, *War on Two Fronts,* 128n.

40. Philip Needham, "The Schizophrenia of an Army: A Diagnosis and a Proposed Solution," unpublished paper from 1966.

41. Frederick Coutts, quoted in Harry Dean, "The Dynamic Centrality," *The*

Officer (August 1972), p. 359.

42. Frederick Coutts, quoted in Sallie Chesham, *Born to Battle: The Salvation Army in America* (New York: Rand McNally, 1965), p. 183.

43. John D. Waldron, ed., *Creed and Deed: Toward a Christian Theology of Social Services in The Salvation Army* (Oakville, Ontario: The Salvation Army Triumph Press, 1995).

44. In that volume, Philip Needham argues for a "Re-integration of the Salvationist Mission." He suggests that one should consider biblically mandated social responsibility; the Salvation Army's Wesleyan heritage in line with Wesley's own paradigm, "Acts of Piety and Mercy"; the Salvationist commitment to holistic ministry; and contemporary theology's emphasis on *koinonia* and eschatological hope. He suggests three paradigms for Salvation Army social work: an overflow of Christian caring, social service as sacrament, and "two arms, and one task," with the one task being redemption and the two arms being evangelism and social services.

45. That is certainly not the case for every person in the field of "social work." But it is true that In The Salvation Army, social work is not necessarily seen as an essential Christian practice but a "profession" and a "department" rather than something vital to Christian identity.

46. This phrase, "temporal salvation," was used by William Booth in his book *In Darkest England* as a way to describe salvation in terms that could be broadly understood as social salvation.

47. William Booth, *In Darkest England,* p. 24.

48. See Pohl, *Making Room,* pp. 61–84.

49. William Booth, *In Darkest England,* p. 44.

50. Catherine Booth, "Compel Them To Come In," *East London Evangelist: A Record of Christian Work Among the People, an Organ of the East London Christian Mission* (March 1, 1869): 81. Quoted in David Rightmire, *Sacraments and The Salvation Army*, p. 189.

51. Catherine Booth, quoted in Bramwell Booth, *These Fifty Years* (London: Cassel, 1929), pp. 45–46.

52. Bramwell Booth, *Papers on Life and Religion* (London: The Salvation Army, 1920), p. 125.

53. William Booth, quoted in Sandall, 3:59; Fairbank, p. 184; Philip Needham, "Toward a Re–Integration of the Salvationist Mission" in *Creed and Deed*, ed. Waldron, p. 14.

54. Bramwell Booth, *Echoes and Memories* (London: Hodder and Stoughton), pp. 1–2.

55. James Read, "Notes on Miroslav Volf's Keynote Lecture," *Word and Deed*, vol. 4:2 (May 2002), p. 71.

56. Read, p. 71.

57. Read, p. 72.

58. An outpost is "a locality in which Army work is carried on and where it is hoped a society or corps will develop." *The Salvation Army Year Book 2012* (London: The Salvation Army International Headquarters, 2012), p. 15.

59. Before I began, I had to face and conquer my own biases. Because my spiritual home has been in Salvation Army congregations, and in light of the significant covenant I made as a soldier, I have often thought of the Salvation Army's identity as defined by those who wear uniform as soldiers. I do not think I came to this frame of reference through an

explicit bias toward this segment of Salvation Army ministry; instead, the Army culture has produced this preference in me. But I realized that if I limited the scope of my project to soldiers, the impact of my work would be stunted because it ignored non-soldier members of the congregation and others who were involved in the Salvation Army's ministries.

60. Throughout this book, I refer to "my" leadership or "my" appointment. It is important to note that the office of corps officer is shared with my wife, Captain Abby Miller, who had equal weight in decision-making for the Arlington Corps. Everywhere I say anything about "my" leadership, I could as easily say "our" leadership. But because this project relates specifically to my reflection on my leadership and co-learning through this project, I have chosen to use the first-person pronoun. This usage should not be seen to take away from my theology of female ministry nor the significant role that a husband and wife share in corps officership.

61. I use the broad description "organization" here because there are at least three advisory groups that impact the Arlington Corps: The DFW–Metroplex Advisory Board, the Arlington Corps Advisory Council, and the Salvation Army's North Texas Youth Education Town Council. Within this project, I will refer only to the latter two groups.

62. *The Salvation Army Year Book 2012*, p. 14.

63. Families who reside at the center must have dependent children. Single parents are allowed, but couples who participate must be legally married. The center serves about 160 people a year; the 12,500–square-foot facility can house 15 families at one time.

64. I decided not to include a guest from the shelter on the task force because I wanted to seek the insight of the task force about how we should approach shelter guests and which guests we would seek to include in the session. This proved to be helpful, as guests felt empowered by the session itself, sensing that they had a voice in their own program.

65. First names with last initials are used for most people's names. Where confidentiality could be an issue, names are changed, which is indicated by putting them in quotes on first reference.

66. All the quotes from task force members are taken from a meeting held on Aug. 6, 2011.

67. Quoted in Alan J. Roxburgh and M. Scott Boren, *Introducing the Missional Church: What It Is, Why It Matters, How to Become One* (Grand Rapids: Baker Books, 2009), p. 20.

68. All quotes in this chapter and the next come from the Aug. 20, 2011, session, "Building a Bridge … " transcribed by the author on Sept. 20, 2011.

69. All quotes come from the author's notes of the teen session held on Sept. 15, 2011.

70. George Scott Railton, "Soldier, Rouse Thee!" *The Song Book of The Salvation Army* (London: The Salvation Army International Headquarters, 1987), #693.

More Endorsements for *Holistic Hospitality*

God puts the lonely in families. Andy Miller III is helping us open our arms a little wider, stirring up the love in our hearts to warmly welcome them in Jesus' name.

Stephen Court, Major
Corps Officer, Crossroads Corps
Canada and Bermuda Territory
Twitter: @StephenCourt

Andy Miller III makes a compelling case that hospitality has been part of the Salvation Army's identity, commitments, and practice from the beginning. By providing a strong foundation and a practical model, he shows that in recovering a deeper appreciation of biblical hospitality, it is possible to integrate spiritual and social concerns in a way that is life-giving for all. This book is a wonderful resource!

Dr. Christine D. Pohl, Author
Making Room: Recovering Hospitality as a Christian Tradition
Associate Provost and Professor of Christian Social Ethics
Asbury Theological Seminary
Wilmore, Kentucky

Andy Miller's *Holistic Hospitality* is a clarion call for The Salvation Army to recognize the missional dimensions of Christian hospitality, as rooted in Scripture and tradition. It helpfully examines the historical and theological origins of the Army's social ministry and interprets the same as an expression of William Booth's eschatologically informed "prophetic social ethic." Moving beyond the theoretical, the author provides a practical description and assessment of his model project to implement a hospitality-based approach to ministry in the context of the Army's transitional housing program in Arlington, Texas.

Dr. R. David Rightmire, Author
Sanctified Sanity: The Life and Teaching of Samuel Logan Brengle
(revised, expanded edition, Francis Asbury Press, 2014)
Professor of Bible and Theology, Asbury University
Wilmore, Kentucky

After reading this book, I immediately shared copies with my social service director and the manager of our housing program. It has challenged us to ensure we are doing our best to meet the needs of the whole person in each individual we are privileged to serve. Many thanks to Andy for this great reminder, challenge, and call for us as The Salvation Army to be all we are called to be. I highly recommend this inspiring read to all wishing to move forward in their holistic ministries to those in need of our hospitable service.

Zach Bell, Captain
Corps Officer
Clearwater, Florida

Andy Miller III has provided a splendid vision of hospitality rooted in the Gospel as articulated by General William Booth and the founding pioneers of The Salvation Army. Given how easy it is to collapse the work of God into perfectly good this-worldly action, it is a pleasure to welcome a volume that provides real theological and spiritual foundations for reaching out to the needy. Without these foundations we simply lose heart and energy; with them, we are pulled into a world of divine action that can sustain a lifetime of grinding missionary action.

Dr. William J. Abraham
Outler Professor of Wesley Studies
Altshuler Distinguished Teaching Professor
Perkins School of Theology
Southern Methodist University
Dallas, Texas

Bibically understood, hospitality is not just a social grace. It is a mark of genuine Christian community with definite social implications, and in fact points us to the very character of the Triune God. For this reason I appreciate Andrew Miller's attention to this reality, and the practical way he deals with it. This book, understood and applied, can help the church truly be the body of Christ in today's world.

Dr. Howard Snyder
Wilmore, Kentucky